THE UNITED STATES, SOUTH ASIA AND THE GLOBAL ANTI-TERRORIST COALITION

Anita Inder Singh

India Research Press

India Research Press
B-4/22, Safdarjung Enclave, New Delhi - 110 029.
Ph.: 24694610; Fax : 24618637
www.indiaresearchpress.com
e-mail : contact@indiaresearchpress.com ; bahrisons@vsnl.com

2006

ISBN-10 digit-81-87943-68-8
ISBN-13 digit-978-81-87943-68-6

Cataloguing Publication Data
The United States, South Asia and the Global Anti-Terrorist Coalition
by Anita Inder Singh

Includes references and index.
1. United States : Terrorism, Afghanistan, Pakistan, India
2. Terrorism : United States, Afghanistan, Pakistan, India
3. Security : United States, Afghanistan, Pakistan, India
4. Anti-Terrorism - United States, Afghanistan, Pakistan, India
i. Title   ii. Author

Printed for India Research Press at Focus Impressions, New Delhi-110 003.

Contents

In this book 'South Asia' is defined as India, Pakistan and Afghanistan. The Bureau of South Asian Affairs of the US State Department deals with all three countries.

Introduction

I

11 September 2001. On that fateful day, terrorists belonging to Al Qaeda attacked New York and Washington, in the first direct attack on the territory of the world's only superpower, shattering America's complacency about its impregnable defences, and calling into question the very concept of 'global security'.[1] On 9 October 2004, the news that the Afghans were voting in their country's first-ever election, and their choice of Hamid Karzai as President, were strange and largely peaceful reminders that the war against global terrorism, prompted by 9/11, began in Afghanistan less than five years ago.

What made 9/11 a global event? Perhaps it was the fact that millions of people throughout the world watched the happenings in New York and Washington on their television screens; perhaps it was because 40 per cent of those killed in the attack on the World Trade Center in New York were non-Americans belonging to some eighty countries, making 9/11 a truly international tragedy. Only a large-scale American engagement could contain terrorism, but even as President George Bush vowed to fight it, the US could not win the war alone; it needed different kinds of support from many countries.

II

The Place of South Asia in American Strategy after 2001

South Asia rose in American priorities after 11 September

2001. Probably for the first time since 1945, South Asia is contributing to America's perception of its global primacy and redefinition of its world role. America's war against the Taliban, its perception of India as a country 'poised to shoulder global obligations in cooperation with the United States in a way befitting a major power', and its decision to admit India into the nuclear club in March 2006, all bear this out.[2] The terrorist attacks on New York and Washington originated from an Asian country – Afghanistan. The Taliban, which then ruled Afghanistan, was fostered and sustained by Pakistani government. Also the possession of nuclear weapons by India and Pakistan, together with their long-standing conflict over Kashmir, raises the possibility of a nuclear war between them, or of Pakistan's nuclear arsenal falling under the control of religious extremists trained and sustained by its military. Launching the war against global terrorism, President George Bush averred that the US was fighting, among other things, for freedom. But the American alliances with Pakistan, Uzbekistan and other authoritarian states created considerable scepticism about American goals and the means to achieve them.

From this the following issues arose: what were the security concerns of the US, Afghanistan, India and Pakistan in the war against global terrorism? What did each expect from the post-September 2001 relationship? What were their respective aims? With reference to South Asia, how is the US achieving its aims of fighting terrorism? How clearly defined are its aims? Is it possible to have clearly defined aims in such a 'war'?

The anti-Taliban war established the US as a major political and military power in South Asia. With the sanction of the UN Security Council, it launched a military strike against Afghanistan's Taliban government which had given sanctuary to Osama bin Laden. Joining forces with domestic warlords opposed to the Taliban and using military bases in Pakistan, the US toppled the Taliban in November 2001. Since then there has been no let-up in American efforts to stamp out Al Qaeda and Taliban militants in Afghanistan and Pakistan, and to hunt down bin Laden. To fill the security and political vacuum created by the fall of the Taliban, the US has also underwritten international attempts to stabilise and reconstruct Afghanistan politically, economically and socially.

America's long-term strategy of winning against terrorism may be contradictory to its short-term tactics. Pakistan, which has given the US military facilities against the Taliban, continues to train Islamic militants. The instigator of the 9/11 attacks remains at large, reportedly in Pakistan. Also, the US claimed that it was fighting the Taliban to defend freedom, but it forged its anti-Taliban alliance with Pakistan, which is ruled by General Pervez Musharraf, its fourth dictator since its creation in August 1947. The US claimed to be encouraging democracy in Pakistan. Under American pressure, Musharraf legitimised his dictatorship in a rigged referendum in April 2002, and then consolidated the military's political dominance before holding rigged elections in October 2002. Subsequently, Musharraf announced that he would relinquish his post as Commander-in-Chief in December 2004; only to change his mind. In September 2004, he said he would remain as the army chief and President. He won parliamentary approval in November 2004 to retain both posts until 2007 and preserved the aura of legitimacy.

In the early 1990s, Pakistan created the Taliban with

the US. Then, after 9/11, Pakistan gave the US bases to wage war against that government. The alignment reflected Musharraf's awareness of the political and military implications of America's intent to defeat global terrorism. Islamabad combined with Washington only to ward off an Indo-American alliance, which would have relegated Pakistan to international pariah status. American troops remained in Afghanistan after the fall of the Taliban government, and aligned with the Pakistani army to pursue Taliban and Al Qaeda members in north-western Pakistan. The pursuit continues.

Even as Musharraf claimed that Pakistan had done more than any other country to fight terrorism. Pakistan was accused by both its neighbours, India and Afghanistan, and by international officials, of training militants. America's 'frontline' ally in South Asia is a military man who blocks democracy in his country and is unable or unwilling to check extremist forces trying to destabilise neighbouring India and Afghanistan. Is that because reliance on religious extremists is the only way the military can shore up its political legitimacy?

India is a stable partner which shares democratic values and a desire to see the US contain terrorism in Asia. Because militants trained and sheltered by Pakistan have frequently crossed over the border and committed acts of terrorism in Kashmir, New Delhi and Mumbai, India would like the US to label Pakistan as a state that sponsors terrorism. This Washington has refused to do, but the common interest in containing terrorism has not spoilt the unprecedented friendly relationship between India and the US since September 2001.

Afghanistan is where the fight against the perpetrators

of 9/11 started. That fight continues, as the US, helped by its European allies, tried to create security in Afghanistan to make possible the holding of elections in October 2004. They were glad at Karzai's victory in the presidential election. But security remains to be consolidated in Afghanistan. Security encompasses the fight against terrorism and is a prerequisite for the democratisation and economic progress that are likely to be the best counterpoises to extremism. Only the success of democratisation will mark the failure of terrorism in Afghanistan – so it is in the interest of the US that democracy should take off there.

The post-election era will also call into question American strategy and tactics in Afghanistan. Can security be forged if the US continues to ally with the warlords who challenge the authority of any government in Kabul? Were the elections just an exit strategy, a pretext to avoid responsibility for the political and economic reconstruction of Afghanistan? But without American backing, could any elected Afghan government survive the onslaughts by Al Qaeda and Taliban militants? Has the war against terrorism dragged a willing or unwilling US into a long drawn out engagement in Afghanistan, and more generally, in South Asia?

In December 2004, Afghanistan was the key to routing terrorism and a test-case for democratisation in a Muslim-majority country; Pakistan, the military ally, also a Muslim-majority state, where democracy may remain in a state of permanent gestation; India the supportive and stable democratic friend which would like to see Pakistan designated as a terrorist state – and which will work to strengthen its ties with the US.

All three countries are unique; the uniqueness of each

is a separate strand in a broader American strategy against terrorism, and mirrors the hopes, aims, clarity, unclarity, and contradictions of that strategy. Indeed, the three South Asian countries raise the question whether the US has – or can have – a clearly defined strategy in a war against a stateless enemy that threatens democratic values and security worldwide.

The Elusive

The war against terrorism is a war against an elusive and amorphous enemy. Terrorists are not the uniformed regulars of a national army and, in May 2005, almost four years after the overthrow of the fundamentalist Taliban government of Afghanistan, it is clear that they cannot be defeated by American military action alone. Terrorism is sustained by a global network of money and weapons. Therefore, defeating the Taliban, who provided a safe haven to Al Qaeda, only dealt with part of the problem: it did not imply America's victory in its campaign against terrorism or the capture of Osama bin Laden, the mastermind behind it. Determination to overcome those dilemmas came up against reports, as late as December 2004, that bin Laden was in hiding in Pakistan, on whom the US conferred the status of major non-NATO ally earlier in the year.

Terrorist groups are widely dispersed; they believe they are waging crusades in defence of their religion, and are inspired to fight to death to fulfil their mission. Even the capture of bin Laden would not guarantee the defeat of global terrorism. The US is dealing largely with religious terrorists, whose reach straddles international borders. They see violence as a legitimate means to achieve their divinely

6

ordained ends. They may use force against anyone who is not a member of their group. They include Al Qaeda, the Lebanese Shiite group Hizbullah, the Palestinian Sunni Hamas, and the radical Jewish groups such as Yigal Amir that killed Yitzhak Rabin, the former Israeli Prime Minister, in 1995.

Terrorism can be an ideology of sorts as well as a tool to achieve political power. The teachings of an ancient religion are fused with the technology of globalisation. In South Asia the religious fervour of bin Laden's supporters has been inculcated through *madrasas,* especially in Pakistan; they rally to the call of *jihad* against their enemy, and they are ready to achieve martyrdom through suicide. They have exploited the reach of modern technology to strike and kill at any time, anywhere – in the US, in Europe, in Asia. Terrorism represents the negative side of the 'interdependence' of global society.

In South Asia some of the terrorism is promoted by the state. State-sponsored terrorists are used by some governments as instruments of foreign policy. Pakistan has trained Islamic militants who have crossed over to Afghanistan and Kashmir and committed acts of violence since 9/11. All the militants are not Kashmiris or Pakistanis; many are former Taliban or Al Qaeda members, who, after being defeated by the US in 2001, have turned their guns on other regions.

Terrorist groups have emerged as significant non-state actors in the international system. They have not replaced or changed the traditional concerns of international society, or the international politics between states, but exist with, and challenge them. Also, the instigators of 9/11 threw down the gauntlet before the US, calling its primacy into question. The Bush administration's response to terrorism has in turn raised many questions about American strategy and tactics. For instance, the US gained much international support for its anti-Taliban campaign, which was legitimised by UN Security Council resolutions. But in Iraq[3] some of America's NATO allies questioned the legitimacy and viability of its military operations, while India turned down, in July 2003, an American request for 17,000 soldiers who would combine with American forces there, on the grounds that the American intervention there had not been mandated by the UN[4].

Is Democracy Exportable ?

Washington's alliance with authoritarian states like Pakistan and Uzbekistan drew attention to the 1990s' debates on the desirability and viability of democracy as the basis of the post-Cold War international society. The end of the Cold War and the widespread demand for democracy in Eastern Europe inspired optimism about the chances of building a new order on democratic principles. Democracy was added to the international agenda by the 1993 Vienna Declaration and Programme of Action, and two years later, by the UN Secretary-General's report on *Support by the United Nations System of the Efforts of Governments to Promote and Consolidate New or Restored Democracies*[5]. A resolution passed by the UN Commission on Human Rights in April 1999 underlined that 'democracy, development and respect for all human rights … are interdependent and mutually reinforcing'[6]. Generally speaking, optimism about the subject marked the global *zeitgeist* of the 1990s; some took the view that a 'third wave' of democratisation would spread with amazing speed[7].

As the new millennium gets underway the consolidation of democracy seems to be assured in barely 20 per cent of 'third wave' countries and successful transitions cannot be taken for granted[8]. But this only highlights the importance of democratic values in staving off security challenges to extremism – and why Afghanistan will be a crucial test-case of fighting terrorism to build democracy.

It also raises the old question whether democracy is exportable[9], and of the compatibility of Islam and democracy. Most extremist movements are Muslim, which does not imply that most Muslims are extremists. Most Muslim majority countries are not democratic, but Muslims live as law-abiding citizens of democracies such as India and the United States. Democracy is a Western concept, but so were National Socialism and communism. And communism took off in countries as diverse as Cuba and China; while countries like Spain and Greece had military rulers until the 1970s. European, Christian Belarus shows few signs of becoming democratic. Authoritarian countries with a weak civil society are more likely to be a breeding ground for terrorism, especially if poverty is widespread.

In Pakistan elected governments have often been overthrown by the military. This might appear to support the contention that Islam and democracy are incompatible. But neighbouring India shows that political and religious affiliations and interests are not aligned either for Muslims or the Hindu majority or indeed for any religious community. Afghanistan will be a significant test-case of the compatibility of Islam and democracy[10].

Asia has had only two stable democracies since 1945 – India and Japan. But strong-arm repression in Kashmir has dented (though not weakened) Indian democracy. China, Asia's largest country, is not a democracy. In many other Asian countries democracy has had teething troubles. Unlike in Europe, in Asia there is no strong regional influence favouring democracy. To give just one example, the South Asian Association for Regional Cooperation (SAARC), which includes authoritarian Pakistan and democratic India, does not have democracy promotion on its agenda.

The democratising influences on Afghanistan will probably be India, the United States and its European allies. NATO expanded its presence in Afghanistan in 2005; and Afghanistan is a partner state of the Organisation for Security and Cooperation in Europe. Karzai's own determination to fight the militants sponsored by Pakistan will be an important factor in containing extremism in Afghanistan. So, post-election Afghanistan, being built from scratch, will test the idea that economic generosity, together, if necessary, with military support, can advance democracy in Muslim majority countries. Most states have been forged by war. They include democracies such as the US and the UK – both of which experienced civil wars. But in most of the multi-ethnic post-communist countries there was an absence of war; these showed that democracy and state-building could take off simultaneously. Taken together the absence of war and democratic state-building made the enlargement of the European Union and NATO possible[11].

Democracy and the rule of law are essential for the protection of human rights, and the methods used by the US itself in Afghanistan will simultaneously set an example and reveal the sincerity and ability of the US about building democracy there and more generally, in Iraq and the Middle East[12]. America's war against terrorism in South Asia has a wider international relevance.

Notes

1. There is no agreed consensus on the definition of terrorism. See *A More Secure World: Our Shared Responsibility: Report of the High-Level Panel on Threats, Challenges and Change* (New York: United Nations, 2004), especially paras 157-64.

2. *The National Security Strategy of the United States of America* (Washington 2006), p. 39; Condoleeza Rice, 'The Promise of Democratic Peace: Why Promoting Freedom is the Only Realistic Path to Security', *Washington Post*, 11 December 2005. See also K. Subrahmanyam, 'Indo-US Nuclear Deal: This is an Exceptional Opportunity', *Tribune*, 4 March 2006 and Anita Inder Singh, 'India in US Eyes Democracy is not the only Factor', ibid, 21 March 2006.

    See also Ashley J. Tellis, Michael Wills (eds) *Strategic Asia 2005-06: Military Modernization in an Era of Uncertainty,* (Seattle, WA: The National Bureau of Asian Research, 2005).

3. Ashley Tellis,'Assessing America's War on Terror: Confronting Insurgency, Cementing Primacy' (Seattle, WA: The National Bureau of Asian Research in cooperation with the Carnegie Endowment for International Peace, December 2004). For further discussion on the US and terrorism see Ashley Tellis and Michael Wills (eds) *Strategic Asia: Confronting Terrorism in the Pursuit of Power* (Seattle, WA: The National Bureau of Asian Research), 2004.

4. A discussion on the US and Iraq is beyond the scope of this book. For a stimulating account of differences between Europe and the US see Christopher Coker, 'A Marriage of Inconvenience: The Continuing Rift Between Europe and the United States', *RUSI Journal*, February 2005, pp. 27-32.

5. See Chapter 3 on India.

6. UN General Assembly document A/50/332, 7 August 1995.

7. UN Commission on Human Rights Resolution on Promotion of Democracy, E/CN.4/RES/1999/57, 27 April 1999.

8. Samuel Huntington, *The Third Wave: Democratisation in the Late Twentieth Century* (University of Oklahoma 1991); Robert Bartley,

'The Case for Optimism: The West Should Defend Itself', *Foreign Affairs,* Vol. 72, No. 4, 1993, pp. 15-18.

9.   Thomas Carothers, 'The End of the Transition Paradigm', *Journal of Democracy,* Vol. 13, No. 1, 2002, pp. 6-21.

10. Post-communist Europe inspired analogous debates after the end of the Cold War. Interestingly, Boris Yeltsin, the first elected president in Russia's history, observed that India had 'overturned the stereotype that democracy could work only in conditions of European civilisation'. *Foreign Broadcasting Information Service,* SOV-93-018, 29 January 1993. See also Jacques Barzun, 'Is Democratic Theory For Export?', in Joel H. Rosenthal (ed) *Ethnics and International Affairs: A Reader* (Washington DC 1995), pp. 39-58; Galina Staravoitova, 'Modern Russia and the Ghost of Weimar Germany', in Heyward Isham (ed), *Reading Russia* (Armonk, New York, 1995), pp. 129-45, and Peter Reddaway, 'Russia on the Brink', *New York Review of Books,* 28 January 1993, pp. 30-35.

11. For a fuller discussion of these points, see my 'Only Game in Town', *The World Today,* August/September 2003, pp. 22 - 4. See also Giles Keppel, *The War for Muslim Minds: Islam and the West* (Cambridge MA and London: Harvard University Press, 2004).

12. See my *Democracy, Ethnic Diversity and Security in Postcommunist Europe* (Westport and London: Praeger, 2001).

13. The US accused of Afghan jail deaths, BBC reports, 13 December 2004 and May 2005.

Chapter 1

Afghanistan:
Fighting Terrorism to Build Democracy?

America's war against global terrorism began in Afghanistan, where the Taliban government harboured Osama bin Laden, who masterminded 9/11. The overthrow of the Taliban was intended as the first step in the fight against international terrorism. By November 2001 the Taliban had been defeated and the US, along with its Afghan and European allies, and the UN, devised plans to establish an interim government in Afghanistan as a precursor to elections in 2004. Three years later, the holding of presidential elections – the first in Afghanistan's history – in October 2004 was a success for the US, but what was their significance in the war against international terrorism?

Afghanistan has a population of 26 million, 90 per cent of it is Muslim. The major languages are Pashto and Dari (Persian). Sandwiched between the Middle East, Central Asia and the Indian subcontinent it is bordered by Tajikistan, China, Pakistan, Iran, and Uzbekistan. Geographical location and its own internecine quarrels long made Afghanistan simultaneously a domestic battlefield and the playground of the 'Great Game' between Britain and Russia in the nineteenth century. In 1979 a civil war motivated a Soviet invasion, and Afghanistan became a battleground of the Cold War. Soviet attempts to prop up a pro-communist regime drew the US into a late twentieth century 'Great Game'. Wanting to dislodge the Soviets, the US joined forces with Afghanistan's neighbour, Pakistan, and created the

Taliban to fight the Soviets. The Soviet invasion also soured relations between the governments of Leonid Brezhnev and Indira Gandhi, since India was against the presence of any great power in South Asia.

Unable to end the civil war, subdue Afghanistan and make it a vassal state, and unable to manage their own political and economic perestroika, the Soviets, under President Mikhail Gorbachev, withdrew in 1989. Two years later, the collapse of the USSR and the end of the Cold War left the US as the sole superpower. With post-Soviet Russia becoming NATO's partner for peace in 1994, American interest in Afghanistan declined.

The Taliban stepped into the political vacuum created by the Soviet withdrawal and formed the new government of Afghanistan. Most of the Taliban belonged to the Pashtun majority and controlled about 90 per cent of the country. Their ruthless fundamentalism destroyed the fabric of Afghan society and political culture, and their government was recognised by only three states, including Pakistan.

By the early 1990s, Pakistan saw in its closeness to the Taliban an opportunity to exclude Indian and Iranian influence, and to extend its own, over Afghanistan. Islamabad was of the view that, with the USSR consigned to the mists of history, Pakistan could become a Central Asian power. So, along with Saudi Arabia, Pakistan supported the Taliban[1]. They also nurtured and harboured Al Qaeda. And Osama bin Laden, who allegedly planned – or at least approved of – the attacks on American embassies in Kenya and Tanzania in 1998, on the USS 'Cole' in Aden in 2000, and on New York and Washington on 9/11, today enjoys the protection and hospitality of the Pakistani government. Al Qaeda were held responsible for the attacks, and UN Security Council Resolution 1267 of 15 October 1999 demanded that bin Laden be turned over to the appropriate authorities. Reiterating the demand on 18 September 2001 the Security Council asked the Taliban government to close down terrorist training camps in compliance with its Resolution 1333 of 19 December 2000[2].

The Taliban government, headed by Mullah Muhammad Omar, turned down American demand to give up bin Laden. Omar also rejected a request by Pakistani clerics to hand over bin Laden and suggested that Muslim clerics decide his fate. On 23 September, Omar announced that bin Laden had left Afghanistan[3].

Even as President Bush made clear that the overthrow of the Taliban would be the first move in the war against international terrorism, Mullah Omar called for *jihad* against any American military action. The Taliban was clearly under pressure as Tajik and Uzbek warlords combined to form the Northern Alliance and attacked the Taliban bases on 22 September 2001. On 7 October the US joined forces with the Northern Alliance and launched Operation Enduring Freedom. American cruise missiles and bombers struck at terrorist training camps, air defence systems and airfields in Afghanistan. The campaigns of the Northern Alliance and the US were short and swift: by 13 November the Taliban had abandoned Kabul, which was taken over by the Northern Alliance. The US announced that the Taliban regime had been defeated and toppled.

With the rout of the Taliban, Afghanistan needed peacebuilding, a euphemistic term coined by the former UN Secretary-General, Boutros Boutros-Ghali[4], for building a new state from scratch. America's top priority was to establish security in Afghanistan. This was an uphill task. After more than a quarter of a century of war, Afghanistan was a collapsed state. Afghan warlords, America's allies, were the first to enter the power vacuum and to fill it with their private armies. They would challenge any government established at the centre. Some $27.6 billion were needed for the reconstruction of Afghanistan[5]. Foreign help was essential to increase security, disburse humanitarian aid, set up a functioning administration, create a new social and physical infrastructure and protect human rights.

From the outset it was clear that America's military and economic strength would make it a key player in post-war Afghanistan. The US had two choices: to work for a stable democratic Afghanistan, or one that might be less democratic than wished but might promote development[6]. The first implied expectations which were unlikely to be fulfilled. And the second could not take place without the first. Neither could be achieved without security. Security – or the lack of it – was America's top priority in September 2001, when the Bush administration decided to oust the Taliban; it remained the problem in December 2004, after Hamid Karzai became Afghanistan's first elected president.

The next, related, tasks of the US were to give aid for the reconstruction of the state and to encourage the formation of a legitimate government. Washington did not want to take the responsibility for either of these. State reconstruction meant providing the resources and expertise to introduce human rights norms, judicial and constitutional commissions; to build an accountable and transparent government, based on the rule of law, which could underpin the economic progress necessary to tackle the poverty that is one of the root causes of terrorism. All this required a Marshall Aid Plan for Afghanistan, but there was none. Nor did the US want to have charge of governing Afghanistan. Bush affirmed, on 25 September, that the US would steer clear of nation-building in Afghanistan. Washington's wish to limit its engagement in Afghanistan was in contrast to American strategies after the defeat of Germany and Japan at the end of the Second World War. In Germany American military and civilian personnel restored institutions of local governance, ran everyday administration, distributed food, organised transport and health care. American soldiers were taught how to disarm local police and to interact with the local population. In both Germany and Japan the US was willing to station troops over an extended period; in fact they remained for seven years. US garrisons controlled the whole of Japan, and, along with their British and French allies, three out of four military sectors in Germany[7].

In Afghanistan America's long-term strategy of forging security sometimes seemed to be at odds with its tactics and choice of allies. Necessity compelled the US to combine with the Northern Alliance to defeat the Taliban; neither the Americans nor the Alliance could have achieved that on their own. For the warlords, too, expediency forged the anti-Taliban compact. In siding with the US the warlords were not motivated by the desire to consolidate security, let alone introduce democracy. In 2001 the power vacuum after the defeat of the Taliban gave the warlords the chance to carve out personal fiefdoms, and, at times, America's 'post-Taliban' collaboration with them only seemed to increase instability.

Afghanistan is divided into 34 provinces[8], which are subdivided into *hauzas*. The *hauzas*, created by the Soviets, formed the bases of the warlords, who exercised a combination of military, political and economic power outside any constitutional framework. Historically the central government had been weak in Afghanistan. With the help of Pakistan's intelligence services, the US fought the Soviets by giving arms and money to several Afghan military commanders, thereby facilitating the rise of warlordism. After 9/11, Pakistan was America's conduit to the warlords. So the warlords continued to fight for territory and power, not just against the Taliban. Perhaps fearful that they might lose power after the October 2004 elections, perhaps hoping to use the elections as a chance to preserve or expand their own political base, strong military leaders, within and outside Hamid Karzai's government, jostled to secure a political vantage point through military means, perpetuating instability in Afghanistan.

The warlords also had economic reasons to create their own fiefs. Afghanistan produces three-quarters – some 3,600 tons-of the world's opium. Half of Afghanistan's GNP (Gross National Product) is earned through a $2.5 billion opium – trade. The end of the Taliban government saw an increase in the growth of poppies in the areas controlled by the warlords, even as they helped the US to hunt bin Laden and members of Al Qaeda and the Taliban. Apparently the Bush administration turned a blind eye to the involvement of its warlord friends in local wars and the narcotics trade. The production of opium poppies filled the warlords' coffers with the cash to buy weapons: their annual income from this was estimated at about $2.3 billion, or almost eight times the government's tax revenues. Indeed, opium production actually increased by two-thirds in 2003-04[9].

Much of the opium produced in Afghanistan ends up

in Europe, through Central Asia and the Caucasus, including Chechnya. Some of these areas are also rich in oil and gas. Ninety per cent of the heroin that makes its way into Britain comes from Afghanistan. Within Afghanistan, the warlords control the routes through which the opium is transported to foreign countries. These routes are also used for cross-border infiltration by terrorists financed by Saudi Arabia and trained by Pakistan. The warlords controlled the major customs posts, including Kandahar, Herat, Jalalabad and Balkh, through which goods were smuggled into Pakistan. The warlords strengthened their authority through smuggling, trafficking in drugs and illegal transit fees.

Following the defeat of the Taliban, American priorities included the consolidation of security, peace-building, demobilisation, disarmament, and preparing the ground for presidential and parliamentary elections. Not wanting to administer Afghanistan the Bush administration was receptive to a suggestion made, on 13 November, by Lakhdar Brahimi, the UN Secretary-General's Special Representative for Afghanistan, that a conference of Afghan representatives be held, and an interim authority be created, under UN auspices. This strategy rightly mirrored the idea that only a government enjoying popular legitimacy could set priorities and build peace.

As a first step, the UN convened a conference in Bonn in November 2001. The Bonn Conference brought the warring Afghan factions to the negotiating table, urged them to overcome the prevailing culture of violence in a country that had experienced more than two decades of civil war, and where armed groups, equipped and financed by neighbouring countries, resolved all disputes by force. By 29 November the Northern Alliance in Bonn had consented to an international peace-keeping force in Afghanistan. On 20 December UN Security Council Resolution 1386 authorised the creation of the International Security Assistane Force (ISAF) to police Afghanistan[10]. On 23 May 2002 the UN Security Council extended ISAF's mandate until December 2002[11].

The negotiators at Bonn were concerned at the instability caused by the warlords belonging to the Northern Alliance, who, emboldened by their success in routing the Taliban, emerged able to challenge any central government that tried to diminish their power. But the warlords could not be ignored or replaced in any peace process. There could be no consensus without them; only by inclusion could the warlords be persuaded to take part in the forging of consensus. The Afghan delegates also included supporters of the former king, Zahir Shah, Pashtuns reportedly supported by Pakistan, and non-Pashtuns said to be close to Iran.

There was much debate at the Bonn Conference about the powers of the central and provincial governments. Afghanistan needed a strong centre at least for defence and foreign policy. But would the warlords opposed to it take responsibility for humanitarian assistance or providing security for officials working for international agencies?

A negotiation of powers between a centre and provincial governors could only be made in a peaceful environment. The Bonn Agreement of 5 December 2001[12] provided for the establishment of a *Loya Jirga,* tribal grand council, in Kabul in June 2002. The *Loya Jirga* then suggested an interim administration that would last for two years and framed security arrangements. The *Loya Jirga* chose Hamid

Karzai as Chairman of the transitional administration on 13 June 2002. Washington announced that the US Special Forces would provide security to Karzai. His government was not chosen by secret ballot but through secret negotiations. Under UN Security Council Resolution 1383 of 6 December 2002 the *Loya Jirga* aimed to create a broad-based, multi-ethnic and fully representative government.

The very formation of the *Loya Jirga*, after 23 years of war, was an achievement of sorts. The *Loya Jirga* comprised groups that had taken part in Operation Enduring Freedom. Dialogue appeared to have replaced war as a way of state-building. But the power of the warlords was obvious. They were major stakeholders in the *Loya Jirga*; they interfered with decision-making and chose most of the delegates. Compromise meant that Karzai include several warlords in his government who were responsible for human rights abuses as provincial governors or as members of the police; for instance, General Abdur Rashid Dostum, a powerful Uzbek warlord, faced allegations of human rights violations. But if human rights and democracy were placed on the agenda, how could they be advanced or safeguarded in the absence of a strong central authority? Karzai also had to contend with the ethnic and political fault lines that divided the *Loya Jirga*.

The *Loya Jirga* governed from June 2002 until 2004. It oversaw the formation of a national army, prepared for elections at the end of its term, and, by 5 January 2004 it had drafted a constitution. The constitution provided for strong presidential powers, including the power to veto legislation, appoint ministers and Supreme Court judges, subject to the approval of the lower house of parliament. The draft constitution also envisaged the creation of a bicameral legislature, with a directly elected lower-chamber and an indirectly chosen upper house. The president had the authority to appoint a third of the members of the upper house and half of those appointees would be women[13].

Karzai's first task was to stabilise the country, but his writ hardly ran outside Kabul[14]. The US appears to have kept a foot in both camps: supporting Karzai but helping – or at least overlooking-the belligerence of the warlords. This implied insufficient military aid to Karzai and a limited engagement in Afghanistan. To capture members of the Taliban, the US worked with the warlords, including Abdul Rashid Dostum, Ismail Khan, the governor of Herat, and Gul Agha Sherzai, the governor of Kandahar, all of whom had their own foot-soldiers. Ismail Khan headed a militia of some 30,000 and controlled lucrative customs posts on the borders with Iran and Turkmenistan. In August 2003 he refused to disband his private armed force or step down as provincial military commander under a rule that he could not hold civil and military positions simultaneously. Karzai also failed to persuade Gul Agha Sherzai and Abdur Rashid Dostum to dismantle their militia in return for posts in the central government.

The complexities and contradictions inherent in this strategy were evident before the October 2004 elections. Many warlords challenged the authority of Karzai, whom the Bush administration wished to see elected as president in 2004. Karzai himself vowed not to include recalcitrant warlords in a post-election government, if he were elected president. But giving them the sack could provoke turbulence. Seeking to expand his authority over the country before polling day on 9 October, Karzai ousted Ismail Khan on 12 September as governor of Herat. His boldness triggered a spate of violence, including an attack on the local UN office, which led UN personnel to leave the city.

The results of these messy compromises with truculent, feuding warlords were clear even after the elections – security remained the greatest challenge to the emergence of peace and democratic processes and to the stability of Afghanistan. The problem was not confined to military issues, it extended to the narcotics trade, border and customs control, structural economic reforms, building roads, within Afghanistan and between Afghanistan and neighbouring states. Insecurity meant that foreign countries would be reluctant to invest in Afghanistan. By colluding with both the Karzai and warlord camps, the US actually worked against the inclusive democracy and the very stability that it sought in Afghanistan.

The US was unwilling to be mired, 'Vietnam style', into Afghanistan. But the warlords could not be disarmed by Karzai or the UN alone. Washington dragged its feet when it came to paying the cost of stability, defeating terrorism and building democracy. Prior to the elections, Karzai had to negotiate with the warlords. The dialogue continued after his electoral victory. Much will depend on how much economic assistance he receives from international donors. That aid will provide him with the resources needed to persuade the warlords to play ball with the centre and build stable political coalitions.

The domestic causes of tension had to be addressed since international conflicts often have internal roots. In general, then, security and the formation of a legitimate state were the needs of the hour, for terrorism flourishes in the absence of stability. War had to be followed by confidence-building measures (CBMs).

Internationally, after October 2001, the US was, and will remain, the main foreign player in Afghanistan. Europe is also involved, through ISAF. Afghanistan is a partner country of the Organisation for Security and Cooperation in Europe (OSCE). Soon after the 2004 elections, ISAF announced that it would increase its strength in Afghanistan in 2005 and extend its reach throughout the country. It may combine with American troops to create a single force[15].

Meanwhile, Karzai tried to rebuild good relations with neighbouring countries through the Kabul Declaration on Good Neighbourly Relations in December 2002. This was in the first instance a pledge by Afghanistan's neighbours, including China, Iran, Pakistan, Tajikistan, Turkmenistan and Uzbekistan to respect its sovereignty and territorial integrity, and to collaborate in the interdiction of the narcotics trade.

What else could be expected from them? A nation-state itself, Pakistan played the ethnic card to stake its claim to influence Karzai's government and the US by stating that Pashtun interests must be safeguarded, without spelling out how. Pashtuns straddle the Afghan-Pakistani border; many of the Taliban were Pashtuns. Pakistan equates the alignment of territory, ethnicity and political identity and interests: for Islamabad the territorial and ethnic nations are synonymous. The logic of the nation-state goes against the grain of building a multi-ethnic Afghanistan. For, if ethnic division equals political division there can be no meeting ground between tribes; no attempt to bridge political differences and forge the consensus which is simultaneously a means to achieve stability and an end in itself[16]. 'Divide and rule' has been practised by authoritarian rulers, imperial and non-imperial, to prevent the formation of any political merger against them. Playing the ethnic card will not promote democracy or unity in Afghanistan any more than it has in Pakistan. Islamabad's stress on ethnic mobilisation of the Pashtuns will only thwart the emergence of the multi-ethnic democratic arrangement that the US wants to see taking root in Afghanistan. Unable to build democratic consensus at home, Islamabad will not be a democratising influence in Afghanistan. Its military and intelligence train extremist groups, some of whom have tried to assassinate Musharraf himself. Inspired by the ideology of the nation-state, Musharraf has appeared unable or reluctant to stop such training at home and has certainly not tried to end their activities against India; and he is unlikely to contain them in Afghanistan[17]. On the contrary, Pakistan may try to use militants living in its territory bordering Afghanistan to put pressure on Karzai in case he tries to get too close to India for Pakistan's comfort. An unstable Pakistan will be a factor for destabilisation in Afghanistan.

Karzai, on the other hand, was critical of Pakistan's involvement in training the militants who crossed over from Pakistan into Afghanistan. On 5 and 15 September 2004, he escaped assassination bids by the Taliban. International officials, including Zalmay Khalilzad, then American Ambassador in Kabul and Lakhdar Brahimi, the UN Special Representative in Afghanistan, both echoed Karzai's allegations against Pakistan[18]. But the Bush administration continues to praise Pakistan's help in stamping out terrorism[19].

Iran supported Ismail Khan in Herat; Russia helped Muhammad Fahim in the north-east. Afghanistan's authoritarian – or illiberal – neighbours will not be able to help its democracy. India strengthened trade links and offered economic and electoral assistance, but the extent to

25

which it can be a democratising influence is uncertain. More importantly, perhaps, Karzai must have the carrots and sticks necessary to advance democracy and development. The onus for that – whether in terms of forging stability or presenting a substantial economic package to sustain it – will fall on the West, in particular on the US.

What, then, does American economic aid reflect about its commitment to the reconstruction of Afghanistan? Of the estimated $27.6 billion needed to rebuild Afghanistan the US pledged $296 million in 2002, the EU and Japan $500 million each, India and Pakistan $100 million each, Iran $560 million and Saudi Arabia, $220 million. India and Pakistan were, therefore, unlikely to be major players in Afghanistan. Iran and Saudi Arabia could emerge as strong influences, with the nature of their influence uncertain. Of the $4,560 billion aid allocated in 2002 by the US, only $90 million was given to Karzai's government to support its activities. But by mid-2003 the US had made up these deficiencies as part of the $87 billion aid package for Iraq and Afghanistan. Most of the aid – some 80 per cent – was spent on relief programmes rather than reconstruction[20].

As the largest donor, Washington would probably have the most leverage over any government in Kabul; the US, Europe and Japan together would probably be the major aid givers; and stability would largely depend on them.

Security will be a major preoccupation of the American and Afghan governments. Security has always been precarious, but there are some grounds for optimism. Since the fall of the Taliban government in November 2001, neither the Taliban nor Al Qaeda have launched large-scale attacks.

Neither tried to disrupt polling on 9 October 2004. There has been no relapse into civil war. By 2003 more than two million refugees had returned and the creation of a national army was underway.

'Insecurity' comprised attempts to kill Karzai, the gunning down of Chinese workers in June 2004, involvement in the drugs and arms trades. The defeat of the Taliban and the breakup of Al Qaeda network in Afghanistan were merely the first essential moves towards building security. They were pyrrhic victories. Al Qaeda and Taliban fighters- their numbers unknown – remained elusive, and mopping up operations continued throughout the tenure of the interim administration. There were reports of new training camps opened by Al Qaeda. The warlords helped the US to hunt down the Taliban and Al Qaeda but their militia terrorised civilian populations. Power struggles between rival militia were common. In 2003 skirmishes in Mazar-i-Sharif between fighters of Uzbek military commander Abdur Rashid Dostum and the Tajik commander Atta Muhammad only ended under international pressurex[21]. Attacks by the Taliban fighters continued after the elections, again highlighting the need for the US to give Karzai the help needed to make his administration strong and secure.

Within the cabinet there was infighting between reformist and more conservative ministers. This sometimes blocked the introduction and implementation of political and administrative reform. On 28 January 2002, Bush committed the US to training a new national army and police force for Afghanistan, but it was several months later, on 2 December 2002, that the Afghan National Army was created by presidential decree. A state must have a monopoly of force, so, not surprisingly, the decree outlawed private militia.

For several reasons this was easier said than done. The mistrust and rivalry among military commanders stalled demobilisation of their forces and the establishment of a national army[22]. Ethnic differences, combined with the desire for political power, prevented the development of a new army. The fact that the Ministry of Defence was in charge of both the national army and the Afghan militia forces hardly helped. Muhammad Fahim, the Defence Minister, filled the Defence Ministry with his fellow Tajiks and kept the strength of the new Afghan National Army down to a mere 7,500 troops instead of the 40,000 it needed to extend the centre's authority. Fahim also maintained about 30,000 private troops in Kabul and turned down international requests to demobilise them. Barely 5 per cent of his foot-soldiers were disarmed before the elections. In the south and south-east, where the Taliban and Al Qaeda were strong, militia were needed to fight against them[23]. A plan to train a Pashtun force for military action in southern and eastern Afghanistan fell through because General Basilar Khan, a Tajik, opposed its formation. Another militia was headed by the Agriculture Minister, Sayyid Hussain Anwari. New militia, their strength unknown, were continually created and equipped with new weapons. The UN wanted 40 per cent of all militia to be disarmed before the elections. This would have involved the decommissioning of whole divisions. Fahim countered that the size of each militia be reduced by 40 per cent while leaving their structure and the authority of their respective commanders intact[24]. Fahim would not reduce divisions loyal to him: their strength increased his standing during the election campaign. Disarmament remained incomplete in December 2004.

A multi-ethnic force could only be created with outside help. To counter the Tajiks the US set up recruitment centres in Kabul, Jalalabad, Gardez, Banyan and Kandahar in the hope of building a more ethnically diverse army. But that was not enough: the ANA had a desertion rate of 10 per cent. With the political situation in a state of flux military commanders were fearful that a national army would reduce their power and were unwilling to surrender arms. The strength of militia hostile to Karzai was unknown – it could have been as high as 90,000[25]. Internecine struggles within groups or between the warlords exacerbated tensions.

Even as preparations for elections were made, warlords threatened Karzai with violence and Karzai sought more troops from NATO as the security situation in Afghanistan worsened[26].

More generally, security threats loomed large in the run-up to the 2004 elections, and problems in organising the elections reflected the instability and problems of state-building in Afghanistan. Taliban insurgents, some crossing over from Pakistan, and militia belonging to the Hizb-i-Islami, loyal to Gulbuddin Hikmatyar, tried to disrupt the registration of voters[27]. There were skirmishes between commanders supported by Karzai's government and warlords refusing to disarm. Electoral workers and candidates were attacked, time and again, leading the EU and OSCE to refrain from sending full-fledged observation missions. A rocket attack on Karzai's helicopter on 16 September 2004 forced him to abandon his campaign in south-eastern Gardez. At one point a frustrated and embattled Karzai observed that the warlord militia were a bigger problem than the Taliban because they were undermining the building of institutions in Afghanistan[28].

NATO's failure to establish its own garrisons around the country reflected its failure, and that of American troops, to dismantle the competing militia maintained by local warlords or to build a viable national army under the central government's command. The Japanese funded a project to disarm, demobilise and reintegrate about 40 per cent of the Northern Alliance forces that helped America to defeat the Taliban. But the low wages offered to the militiamen to give up their weapons and to disband their troops offered little incentive, and the programme fizzled out.

The 8,500 ISAF forces were concentrated around Kabul. Even in Kabul the warlords did not demilitarise their forces. Outside Kabul, warlords appeared to have carved up the country amongst themselves. Some 40,000 Afghan police guarded polling booths; they were buoyed by ISAF and about 14,000 troops from the new-born Afghan National Army. The US moved its own troops, operating independently of ISAF, to the Afghan-Pakistani border to check infiltration from Pakistan. Most of the 20,000 American troops in Afghanistan concentrated on pursuing the Taliban in the southern part of the country. Some politicians were worried that the polls, which were supposed to result in new political arrangements for Afghanistan, might fall prey to the warlords and criminal gangs, determined to protect their fiefdoms. Nascent political parties could not compete with provincial governors who had guns. Registration for the elections was slow; Karzai could not issue electoral laws delineating the boundaries of electoral constituencies. Fundamentalist leaders, fearful of losing influence in a new political dispensation, obstructed the activities of political parties.

Elections were postponed twice. The Bonn Agreement envisaged that elections would take place in June 2004, but on 28 March 2004, Karzai announced the holding of simultaneous presidential and parliamentary elections in September. Later it was decided that presidential elections would take place in October 2004, parliamentary elections in April 2005. Low voter registration was part of the reason for the postponement, and a draft electoral law still did not outline the electoral constituencies. This was eventually done by presidential decree on 5 June 2004. The constituencies had to be redefined to address some deficiencies before the provincial and parliamentary elections in 2005. Because of continuing security considerations, they were postponed till September 2005.

By August Karzai had announced the registration of more than eight million voters. There were multiple registrations of voters. This is often the case in post-conflict countries but in Afghanistan it reflected the lack of security. In the Taliban stronghold of Panjshiri the number of cards given was two and a half times the registered number of voters. The militia tried to bully people into voting for their warlord. Voters were not registered in the south and east of Afghanistan, areas destabilised by militants crossing over the border from Pakistan[29].

Insecurity made it difficult to lay the foundations of inclusive democracy. Afghanistan's draft constitution grants the right to form political parties within certain limits. Understandably enough, parties having 'military or quasi-military aims and organisation' were barred from contesting the elections. So were parties whose manifestoes and charters contravened 'the Holy religion of Islam'[30].

What did this mean in practice? For example, women registered to vote, but the stress on Islam could be interpreted to mean they should not. Communal parties, based on religion, language and religion could not participate – which could please any advocate of multi-ethnic parties. But this limited the intellectual and political choice that is inherent in democracy[31].

Most of the 27 odd political parties were unable to meet the criteria to be recognised as political parties. Some of Karzai's own cabinet colleagues put pressure on parties not to register. The qualifications and competence of members of the Joint Electoral Management Body (JEMB) and its effectiveness were also in question. Members of the JEMB were selected by Karzai, casting doubt on their impartiality. But even if the allegations about lack of partiality were correct it could be asked what alternatives he had, given the fragile democratic traditions and the militant opposition he faced, at times from his own cabinet colleagues.

Karzai himself cultivated the support of his fellow Pashtuns. This may have reflected the absence of consensus in Afghanistan. Karzai will have to reconcile Afghans divided along ethnic and political lines, enlarge his political base and enhance his national standing. The interest of the Pashtuns in a strong centre, may not be shared by the Hazaras and Uzbeks, who have little tradition of participating in central governments and may resist what they see as Pashtun dominance. Politics is the art of the possible: much will depend on how inclusive Karzai can make his post-election government. That, in turn, will hinge on the incentives he can offer politicians and the military to work as a team in a democratising government.

Ethnic and political alignments divided the central government. Within the *Loya Jirga* itself, Karzai faced.

opposition. For instance, Karzai challenged by Ahmad Massoud (Panjshiri), who approached Shia parties to field a common candidate for the presidential election. The ousting of Ismail Khan, the Governor of Herat, in September 2004, was probably intended to reduce his challenge to the centre.

Even after Karzai's victory in the presidential election, he had to deal with the warlords who controlled private armies, police and intelligence sources and gathering of revenues. ISAF and American soldiers, therefore, had to have the resources and strength to help Karzai counter warlords and to promote disarmament and demobilisation. Karzai is determined to fight warlords and will not court them. Warlords continued to control local police and have had the capacity to intimidate election workers, candidates and voters. Attempts were made to persuade military commanders to disarm their forces by making their registration for parliamentary elections in 2005 contingent on demilitarisation[32].

Peace-building in Afghanistan will be a long haul. The difficulties inherent in establishing the security needed to make the peace process fully inclusive were evident at the time of the Bonn Agreement. After the elections, demilitarisation and disarmament made slow progress because the centre and ISAF lacked the means to carry them out[33].

Karzai's electoral triumph in October 2004 gave him time to expand his power base before parliamentary elections in 2005. He has yet to consolidate his authority outside Kabul. Demobilisation and disarmament were not completed before the parliamentary elections in September 2005. The expansion of ISAF in 2005 did not stop a rise in extremist violence in 2005. Security is a prerequisite for the development of democratic norms and to build stable political institutions. These in turn sustain the institutions through which all sections of Afghan society can articulate their wishes. But there is little debate about new administrative and political institutions. ISAF's presence remains necessary to deter the warlords, but would it be prepared for a long drawn out engagement necessary to consolidate democracy in Afghanistan? Only a determined effort by Karzai, supported by ISAF and the Afghan National Army, will ensure the disarmament of the militia.

A wish to build political coalitions, intertwined with the desire to prevent the Taliban and Hizbullah-i-Islami from disrupting the parliamentary polls motivated Karzai to offer amnesty to moderate Taliban who laid down arms. Taliban not accused of criminal acts could join the peace process and be treated like 'ordinary Afghans'[34]. That may be easier said than done. In the wake of Karzai's electoral success there was a spate of attacks by recalcitrant Taliban fighters against his government, the United Nations Assistance Mission in Afghanistan (UNAMA), and clergy engaged in organising the parliamentary elections. Most of the Taliban and Hikmatyar's supporters were trained and paid by Pakistan's intelligence services[35]. American pressure on Islamabad to stop terrorist activities seemed to have little effect.

Afghan paramilitary forces, earning better salaries than their compatriots in the Afghan national army, obstructed American efforts to find Taliban and Al Qaeda members. But did hunting the Taliban really make them anti-terrorist or did it give them a pretext to continue using arms and perpetuating the culture of violence? A state must have a monopoly of violence. Karzai's Afghanistan has still to fulfil that condition. He would need much more military and economic assistance to create that monopoly. Only then can the rule of law and economic development make headway. American generosity or tight-fistedness will be the litmus test of its determination to defeat terrorism.

The enhancement of security and the bringing of warlords under control will also entail the curbing of the narcotics trade. The drugs trade has adversely affected Afghan politics. In 2004 opium cultivation increased in all the provinces of Afghanistan. Eighty-seven per cent of the world's illegal crop was grown in Afghanistan; farmers and drug dealers earned some $2.8 billion, which was the equivalent of 60 per cent of the country's GDP in 2003. Access to money from drug trafficking partly explained the refusal of warlords to disarm their foot-soldiers. Income from narcotics had also funded the Taliban. Not surprisingly, Karzai placed the battle against drugs high on his agenda. He will need international help to win this fight. The police and army lack the resources necessary to deal with the different links in the chain of narcotics production[36].

The parliamentary elections held in 2005 also entailed the curbing of warlords and the disarmament of their militiamen to prevent commanders with militia from terrorising villages, reducing the elections to a farce and producing a parliament comprising armed men[37].

Did Karzai's election as president strengthen democratic forces? It is too early to say. But the acceptance of the election results by his militarised opponents suggested at least a willingness to play by the first rule of the democratic game. The decision of Yunus Qanouni to form a political party to contest the parliamentary elections in 2005 mirrored a willingness to try to gain power through the ballot box rather than through guns.

Nevertheless, security will remain at the top of the political and military agendas – for Karzai and for the US. Elections cannot be an exit strategy for the US: rather Washington must increase military and economic aid to Karzai to strengthen his position, to have more carrots – and if necessary sticks – to negotiate and bargain successfully after the elections, to make the political dialogue among Afghan politicians as constructive as possible. Karzai will need military support to contain warlordism and to sustain the process of peace-building that has been given a fillip by the presidential elections.

Having supported the warlords out of political expediency before the elections the US must now help Karzai to build a strong centre. Karzai is determined to curb warlordism: will the US give him the help he needs? In his cabinet, announced on 7 December 2004, technocrats were included at the expense of warlords and religious leaders.

Karzai will simultaneously have to overcome, and work with, the tribal divisions among his cabinet colleagues. He must counter the possibility of Pakistan exploiting any discontent among the Pashtuns. Pakistan harped on the theme that they had lost out after 9/11 and that Pakistan wanted to help them. That propaganda made little impression on Pashtuns in Afghanistan, who made no moves for cross-border Pashtun unity – which worked to Karzai's advantage. Karzai won in the areas bordering Pakistan, including Kandahar, Kabul, Patoka, and border provinces, which had been the stronghold of warlords, including Herat, Balkh and Kundnz. He won more than 90 per cent of the vote in many Pashtun provinces, 60 per cent in Wardak and 53 per cent in Ghazni, which extend into Hazara areas. In mixed areas such as Farsawan and Herat, his margin was lower but he still obtained the majority of votes. Yunus Qanouni, his main rival, failed to consolidate his base among his own Tajik community. In the Tajik-majority province of Badakshan, Karzai won more than half the vote. But he has yet to win over the Hazaras in the central highlands, and also in Kabul. A large share of the Uzbek vote went to Ahmad Rashid Dostum. Uzbeks and Tajiks now control areas once dominated by the Taliban.

Braving intimidation from militia and militants, Afghan voters turned out in large numbers to vote. Even if allowances were made for electoral irregularities, Karzai won a decisive mandate to foster democratic governance. But elections to the National Assembly and Provincial Council, held against a background of increasing extremist violence on 18 September 2005, dampened optimism about Afghanistan's transition to democratic stability[39]. Afghanistan's new parliament, its first in three decades, comprises former warlords, reconciled Taliban commanders, urban professionals, communists and three mujahiddin parties, but most of its members are political moderates.

The reconstruction of Afghanistan remains an uphill climb. The Afghanistan Compact, signed at the London Conference on Afghanistan on 31 January 2006, envisages measures ranging from the disbandment of militia and the creation of an efficient police force to the recognition of property rights. Maintaining its level of aid the US has promised to give $1.1 billion in 2007. ISAF will spread out from Kabul to southern, northern and eastern Afghanistan and merge with an American-led force of 20,000 troops. But extremist violence, originating from bases in Pakistan, has risen over the last year, and at least 30 suicide bomb attacks have taken place. Renewed American attacks on terrorist bases in Pakistan only provoked anti-American protests there. The complexities of the war on terror have been exacerbated by armed resistance to officials trying to snuff out the opium trade. Corrupt officials, governors and judges relegate democratic progress and accountability to a distant future.

The outstanding reality is that Karzai must build a new political and economic infrastructure that will lay the foundations of long-term peace and development in Afghanistan. His elected government must build up a national army and police force. Illegal armed groups must be demobilised and a healthy civil society developed. The success of state-building through democracy in Afghanistan is necessary for the containment, if not the defeat, of terrorism there.

Notes

1.   Stephen Cohen, 'War and Peace in South Asia', Brookings Institution Analysis paper #10, 21 November 2001.

2.   UN Security Council Resolutions S/RES/1267(1999), 15 October 1999; S/RES/1333(2000), 19 December 2000; S/RES/1368(2001), 12 September 2001; S/RES/1373(2001), 23 September 2001 and S/RES/1378(2001), 14 November 2001.

3.   Entries for 18, 23 and 28 September 2001, USGCAT 2001.

4.   *An Agenda for Peace,* 2nd ed. New York, United Nations, 1995.

5.   *Securing Afghanistan's Future: Accomplishments and the Strategic Path Forward,* 17 March 2004; prepared by the Afghan government and international agencies for the International Conference at Berlin, 31 March-1 April 2004, http://www.cmi.no/afghanistan/background/does/SecuringAfghanistan's Future-18-03-04.pdf.

6.   'Afghanistan and the Challenge of Reconstruction', 17 January 2002, www.ceip.org

7.   Ray Salvatore Jennings, *The Road Ahead: Lessons in Nation Building from Japan, Germany, and Afghanistan for Postwar Iraq* (Washington DC: United States Institute of Peace, April 2003), pp. 27-9.

8.   On 5 June 2004 two new provinces were created by presidential

decree to delineate provincial electoral boundaries before the elections to be held in October 2004. Report to the Secretary-General, *The Situation in Afghanistan and its Implications for International Peace and Security*, A/58/868-S/2004/634, 12 August 2004, para. 10.

9.   Vikram Sood, 'Chaosistan Revisited', *Hindustan Times,* 15 September 2004. See also *The Economist,* 20 November 2004, and *Afghanistan Opium Survey 2004,* United Nations Office of Drugs and Crime, November 2004.

10. UN Security Council S/RES/1386 (2001), 14 November 2001, and S/RES/1413(2002), 23 May 2002.

11. S/RES/1413(2002), 23 May 2002.

12. 'Agreement on Provisional Arrangements in Afghanistan Pending the Restablishment of Permanent Government Institutions', 5 December 2001, and Annexes 1 and 3.

13. Draft Constitution of Afghanistan, Article 35.

14. Afghanistan: Bonn Agreement One Year Later: A Catologue of Missed Opportunities', *Human Rights Watch World Report 2001: Asia.*

15. Final Communique, Ministerial Meeting of the North Atlantic Council held at NATO Headquarters, Brussels, on 9 December 2004, http://www.nato.int/docu/pr/2004/p04-170e.htm.

16. For a fuller discussion of this point, see my *Democracy, Ethnic Diversity and Security in Postcommunist Europe,* especially pp. 8-9.

17. See my 'Pakistan's Dangerous Nation-State Ideal: Democratic Pluralism is the Only Cure for Islamabad's Ills', *Asian Wall Street Journal,* 11 October 2004.

18. *Daily Times* (Lahore), 17 September 2004, and Radio Free Europe/ Radio Liberty Reports, 5 and 25 August 2004.

19. For example, on 4 December 2004 CBS News Report, 'Prez Praises Pakistan Re: Osama', http://www.cbsnews.com/stories/2004/12/07/terror/main659419.shtml.

20. 'The United States and the Global Coalition Against Terrorism (referred to hereafter as USGCAT), September 2001-December 2003, entry for 21 January 2002.

21. Larry Goodson, 'Afghanistan in 2002', *Asian Survey,* Vol. XLIII, No. 1, 2003, p. 183.

22. *Security in Afghanistan,* p. 80.

23. Ibid., and *Situation in Afghanistan,* Para 30.

24. 'Elections and Security in Afghanistan', International Crisis Group Report, p. 3.

25. Michael O'Hanlon, 'Let's Finish the Job in Afghanistan', *The Baltimore Sun,* 13 October 2004.

26. *The Economist,* 16 June 2004.

27. Justin Huggler, 'Afghanistan Hits Fever Pitch As Warlords Turn', *The Guardian,* 6 October 2004.

28. Ahmed Rashid, 'A Vote is Cast Against the Warlords', *Far Eastern Economic Review,* 29 July 2004, and Keith Richburg, 'Karzai Vows to Crack Down on Warlords, Drug Dealers', *The Washington Post,* 5 November 2004.

29. BBC Report, 14 September 2004.

30. Draft Constitution of Afghanistan, Article 35.

31. Ibid.

32. Report of the Independent Expert of the Commission on Human Rights on the Situation of Human Rights in Afghanistan, UN General Assembly doc. A/59/2004, 21 September 2004. See also 'Afghanistan: From Presidential to Parliamentary Elections', International Crisis Group, Asia Report No. 88, 23 November 2004.

33. Report of the Independent Expert on Human Rights on the Situation of Human Rights in Afghanistan, UN General Assembly Document A/59/2004, 21 September 2004, p. 13.

34. Richburg, 'Karzai Vows to Crackdown', *Washington Post,* 5 November 2004.

35. Ahmed Rashid, 'Karzai, Musharraf... New Regional Equations', *The Nation,* 16 October 2004.

36. *The Economist,* 20 November 2004, and *Afghanistan Opium Survey 2004,* United Nations Office of Drugs and Crime, November 2004.

37. Ibid., 30 October 2004.

38. JEMB Election Report, 'Afghan Presidential Elections: By Province', www.electionsafghanistan.org

39. This section is based on *Building on Success: The London Conference on Afghanistan* http://www.unama-afg.org/news/_londonConf/_docs/06jan30-AfghanistanCompact-final.pdf; M.K. Bhadrakumar, 'Has America lost its way in Afghanistan?' *The Hindu,* 17 March 2006; Philip H. Gordon, 'Back Up NATO's Afghanistan Force' *International Herald Tribune,* 8 January 2006; *The Economist,* 5 January 2006, and the excellent *The Situation in Afghanistan and its Implications for International Peace and Security: Report of the Secretary-General,* UN doc.A/60/712-S/2006/145, 7 March 2006. http://www.unama-afg.org/docs/_UN-Docs/_repots-SG/2006/2006-145.pdg.

Chapter 2

Pakistan: Does the Frontline State Help or Hinder the Anti-Terrorist Campaign?

In October 2001 the US began its war against the Taliban regime. Afghanistan's neighbour, Pakistan, ruled by General Pervez Musharraf, the Commander-in-Chief of its army, became an American ally by providing the US with military bases and combining with American troops to hunt the Taliban and Al Qaeda members on its own territory.

Pakistan was a dictatorship in 2001, with sections of the army and intelligence giving overt and covert support to the Taliban. Rigged elections in 2002 preserved the political dominance of the military, which certainly did not join forces with the US in defence of 'freedom'.

Within three days of the attacks on New York and Washington, Musharraf pledged Pakistan's unstinted cooperation in the fight against terrorism. The US saw Pakistan having negligible influence in the Middle East, but Pakistan became a frontline state, partly because it did a 180-degree turn and stopped propping up the Taliban, which it had helped to create in the early 1990s, partly because of its willingness to give bases to the US to wage war against the Taliban. For Pakistan the alignment with the US was vital to pre-empt one between New Delhi and Washington. Musharraf warned his compatriots of very grave consequences if Pakistan did not line up with the US. That would have pushed the US into an alliance with India, which would have been fatal to Pakistan[1].

Musharraf knew that most Pakistanis were opposed to military action against Al Qaeda or the Taliban regime, and he faced a series of anti-American demonstrations after 9/11. Despite the strong wave of anti-Americanism among his countrymen, he allowed the US to launch air strikes against the Taliban from bases at Pasni and Jacobabad. Musharraf's domestic standing rose as the US renewed arms supplies to Pakistan. American weaponry was largely intended to enhance security on the Afghan-Pakistani border.

The events of 11 September 2001 and Musharraf's swift decision to support the US led to a waiving of military sanctions imposed on Pakistan after its nuclear tests in 1998, and the Bush administration resumed military assistance, providing spare parts and equipment to enhance Pakistan's capacity to police its western frontier. On 29 October the State Department announced $1 billion in economic aid to 'strengthen' Pakistan; two years later, President Bush announced that the US intended to provide Pakistan $3 billion in economic and military aid over the next five years[2].

In September 2001, as in June 2006, Pakistan was a worrying ally. The Pakistani state is defined by religion and the danger prevails that popular feeling could turn against Musharraf, or that he could be overthrown by extremist elements or military rivals[3]. Also, there were occasional clashes between American and Pakistani troops jointly pursuing Taliban militants along the Afghan-Pakistani border. How are the US and Pakistan dealing with such problems? What are their implications for American anti-terrorist strategy, in Pakistan and Afghanistan?

Musharraf was an important ally. However, the crucial alignment, for the Bush administration, was with the Tajik and Uzbek warlords in Afghanistan who formed the

Northern Alliance and combined with the US against the Taliban regime. The Northern Alliance started its campaign before the US launched Operation Enduring Freedom on 7 October 2001. Pakistan was concerned that the fall of the Taliban would affect its own influence in Afghanistan, and, even as the Operation gathered pace, Musharraf tried to persuade President Bush and British Prime Minister Tony Blair that 'moderate' Taliban should be included in a new government. Pakistan called for a broad-based government in Afghanistan which would cater to Pashtun interests[4]. This reflected Pakistan's interests in influencing a post-war government. All Pashtuns were not pro-Taliban, but anti-Taliban Pashtuns – like Hamid Karzai – would not be amenable to Islamabad's influence. Meanwhile, the Northern Alliance made known its opposition to the inclusion of any Taliban in a post-war government.

Military reasons prompted Washington to revive its ties with Islamabad after 9/11. During the 1990s, when democracy promotion had ranked relatively high on the American foreign policy agenda, the Clinton administration had cold-shouldered Musharraf since his coup in 1999. In September 2001, President George Bush lauded him as an ally. Musharraf's authoritarian credentials did not matter much at this stage; what counted was his willingness to give the US military facilities that could be used in a war against the Taliban government.

It was not the first alliance between the US and Pakistan: they had a history of military ties. In the early 1950s, Pakistan became an American ally. The Eisenhower administration took the decision to give military aid to Pakistan in January 1954. This marked America's entry into the subcontinent, and its simultaneous replacement of Britain as the dominant power in the region. Britain and the US had divergent geopolitical perceptions of South Asia and the Middle East. The British saw Pakistan as a South Asian power, militarily and economically close to India. The US envisaged Pakistan and Turkey as strategic outposts of the arch of Middle East defence. In 1953 the British knew nothing about American plans to give aid to Pakistan; they were stunned at being kept in the dark about military largesse to Pakistan. Dismayed and indignant at being ignored by the Eisenhower administration they realised that America would don their mantle in the Middle East and South Asia[5].

Pakistan also joined SEATO in 1954 but contributed minimally or in a limited way for American reconnaissance flights on Soviet territory. More generally, in the 1960s, Washington was on excellent terms with the then military ruler, General Yahya Khan, using him as a channel of communication to Beijing, as the Americans tried to establish diplomatic ties with the People's Republic of China. So the US did not condemn Islamabad's 1971 military crackdown in East Pakistan. Instead it criticised the Indian military intervention that resulted in the breakup of Pakistan and the creation of Bangladesh. In a two-week campaign in December 1971, India defeated Pakistan, opening the door to the secession of East Pakistan and the birth of Bangladesh. This military success appeared to confirm India's political and military predominance in South Asia. But not for long: by the end of the 1970s, the Soviet invasion of Afghanistan brought the Cold War on to India's doorstep.

Pakistan's Uses as an Ally

By 2001, Pakistan's highly trained armed forces, numbering more than 620,000, formed the eighth largest army in the world. Pakistan's contiguity with Afghanistan and the

44

Middle East partly accounted for America's interest in its military bases. The US was the largest donor of military and economic aid to Pakistan. Some 40 per cent of the American aid package was disbursed as non-reimbursable credits for military equipment, making Pakistan, after Israel and Egypt, the third largest recipient of American military largesse[6].

The frequent use of Pakistan's army to suppress domestic tensions and perceived opponents of its military rulers, as well as its being in a state of alert for a possible war with India over Kashmir, restricts the extent to which it can be used by the US as a striking force in foreign countries. Musharraf gave military bases to the US but showed no inclination to send Pakistani troops to fight as part of a force led by US in Afghanistan or Iraq.

With the Soviet invasion of Afghanistan in 1979, Pakistan retained its military usefulness to the US. Washington was minded to think that 'Islamic' Pakistan would be a valuable ally against the Soviet Union. Seeking to create a local force that could counter the Soviets militarily and ideologically, the US – along with Pakistan – created the Taliban. The Taliban leadership learned and developed their extremist brand of Islam in *madrasas* in Pakistan. At least 10 to 15 per cent of the *madrasas,* often funded by Saudi Arabia, promoted militant forms of Islam.

In 1989 the Soviets withdrew from Afghanistan. Then, in August 1991, the disintegration of the USSR marked the end of the Cold War. American military interest in Pakistan declined, as the world's only superpower did not need its help against any of the new states that emerged out of the collapsed Soviet Union. The US was embroiled in wars against Iraq in 1991, or in military interventions in the former

Yugoslavia or Somalia. America suspended aid after Pakistan's 1998 nuclear explosion and imposed sanctions after Musharraf staged his coup in 1999. Musharraf was *persona non grata* in Washington. But 9/11 changed that.

To strike at the Taliban, Washington needed military bases and Pakistan could provide them. Alignment with the US during the Cold War had never made Pakistan democratic and until 9/11 Washington did not pretend that they would. Washington perceived Pakistan as an ally of the 'free world' against the Soviet Union, but democracy remained fragile in Pakistan. General Ayub Khan's *coup d'etat* took place in 1958, four years after Pakistan started receiving military aid from the US and joined SEATO. In 1971, General Yahya Khan used military force in East Pakistan because he thought the US would look the other way. Musharraf probably made the same calculation as American officials continually praised him as a moderate Muslim ruler trying to make his country democratic. In 2001, a decade after the end of the Cold War, political expediency again shaped the American perception of Pakistan as an ally of 'freedom'[7].

Is Pakistan a Reliable Military Ally?

Situated in South Asia, Pakistan was created in 1947 as a result of the partition of British India[8] and reflected the desire of the Muslim League to create a homeland for the Muslims of the subcontinent. Pakistan shares borders with India, Afghanistan, and China. With an area of some 803, 943 sq m it has a population of about 145 million, 97 per cent of whom are Muslim. The rest are Christians, Sikhs, Hindus and others. The Muslim population is divided by class and tribe, and the main ethnic groups are Punjabis, Sindhis, Pashtuns,

Baluchis, Muhajirs, the Saraikis and Hazaras. Urdu is the official language; Sindhi, Punjabi, Baluch are significant regional languages. The literacy level is 45 per cent.

Pakistan's definition as an Islamic state has not cemented its ethnic and religious schisms, which have posed serious threats to its territorial integrity[9]. In the mid-1960s, a Baluch uprising was suppressed ruthlessly. Then, in March 1971, the government of Yahya Khan refused to accept election results giving the Awami League a majority in East Pakistan and used strong-arm methods to crush an independent movement. By December the campaign of suppression resulted in 10 million refugees crossing over to India. Despite repeated Indian appeals to Islamabad there was no sign of a reduction in the flow of refugees; this became the *casus belli* for India's military intervention in East Pakistan, which resulted in the breakup of Pakistan and the creation of Bangladesh in December 1971.

The political and social divisions created by Pakistan's diversity did not end with the secession of East Pakistan. Sectarian violence between the Sunni majority and Shia minority had occurred, time and again, since 1947, and violence broke out, yet again, in the aftermath of 9/11. The schism between them has its roots in the differences that emerged after the Prophet's death in 632. The Soviet invasion of Afghanistan and General Zia-ul-Haq's desire to legitimise his military regime prompted him to introduce 'Islamisation' after 1979. These measures actually strengthened hardline Sunnis and enhanced militant influence in politics and society, even as Pakistan, along with the US, created the Taliban to fight the Soviets. Mujahideen, mostly – but not entirely – comprising Sunnis, were trained to eject the Soviets.

After the Soviet retreat from Afghanistan, some

Mujahideen returned home to Pakistan and searched for new causes to wage *jihad*. Pakistan became a well-known base for several terrorist organisations. They included the Lashkar-e-Taiba, the Jaish-e-Muhammad, and the Sipah-e-Sahiba Pakistan. The first two were classified as foreign terrorist organisations by the State Department; the third listed as one of 'other terrorist groups'. The Lashkar-e-Taiba and Jaish-e-Muhammad were described by the UN as 'belonging to or associated with' the Taliban and Al Qaeda[10]. Other mujahideen attacked any Muslims that they regarded as heretics and for Sunni militants that meant the Shia. Sunni extremists belonging to the Sipah-e-Sahiba were allegedly behind attacks on Shia mosques in Quetta and Rawalpindi in March 2002, February 2003 and October 2004. The Sunni-Shia violence gives the military a pretext to make a case for its political indispensability; it also underlines the absence of political or 'Islamic' consensus in Pakistan and exacerbates its domestic instability.

The arrest of Al Qaeda leaders in Pakistan was evidence that they had local protectors. Abu Zubaydah was found in a house belonging to the Lashkar-e-Taiba; four other Al Qaeda suspects had connections with the Jamiat-e-Islami[11].

For some Taliban veterans, Kashmir provided new opportunities. Pakistan remains a breeding and training ground for extremists who have carried out attacks on India and Afghanistan after 9/11. Karzai has alleged that 70 per cent of attacks on Afghan territory have been made by militants trained and based in Pakistan.[12] The 9/11 report on terrorism highlighted Pakistan's prominent role in promoting terrorism[13]. In the 1980s, Pakistan sustained anti-Indian terrorists in the Punjab and Jammu & Kashmir. The alliance with the US has not induced Musharraf's government to renounce terrorism as an instrument of state policy, either in Afghanistan or in Jammu & Kashmir.

The attacks show that extremists remain at large in Pakistan[14]. Al Qaeda, Taliban, Pakistani terrorist groups and sections of the Pakistani military and intelligence are part of a complex international nexus. A network exists against Musharraf himself within the army and intelligence services[15]. The extremists who have tried to kill him are the same people who have attacked Shia mosques and masterminded raids into Indian and Afghan territory. Washington is aware that terrorists connected to Al Qaeda have carried out several attacks in Pakistan since 2001, including two attempts on President Musharraf's life. They also tried to kill Lieutenant-General Ahsan Saleem Hyat, the corps commander of the Karachi area, on 13 June 2004. The attempt on his life took place within 500m of the American consulate and was probably a message for Musharraf and the US. Other attempts to kill senior Pakistani officials included a suicide bomb attack on eight people next to the parked car of Prime Minster-designate Shaukat Aziz in June 2004. Low-ranking Pakistani officers may have instigated the attacks, implying that fomenters of extremism in Pakistan's security service are out of Musharraf's control.

The Bush administration admitted in September 2004 that the containment of terrorism would take a long time, while underlining the need to shut down terrorist organisations and the networks that supported them[16]. But it was persuaded that Musharraf's government was working to achieve this and praised Pakistan in glowing terms:

Three years ago, Pakistan was one of the few countries in the world that recognised the Taliban regime, and Al

49

Qaeda was active and recruiting in Pakistan without serious opposition. Yet the United States was not on good terms with key Pakistani leaders – the very people we would need to help shut down the Al Qaeda operations in that part of the world. Today, the United States and Pakistan are working closely in the fight against terror, and Pakistani forces are rounding up terrorists along their nation's western border. President Musharraf is a friend of our country who helped us capture Khalid Sheik Mohammed, the operational planner behind the 9/11 attacks. Today, because we are working with Pakistani leaders, Pakistan is an ally in the war on terror, and the American people are safer[17].

Earlier, the State Department reported that 77 Pakistani soldiers had lost their lives in anti-terror operations in the tribal areas since the beginning of 2004. Other security personnel had been killed in Karachi and elsewhere, and numerous Pakistani civilians have been murdered in terrorist attacks[18]. Washington knows that there is support for extremists among sections of the Pakistani military and intelligence services; indeed one of the reasons why it supports Musharraf is that nuclear weapons could fall into extremist hands if he were to fall from power[19].

Perceptions of Musharraf

The Bush administration pins its hopes for fighting terrorism on Musharraf, his moderation in political and religious matters, his gift for political manoeuvre and survival. Washington takes the view that Musharraf wants to create a 'progressive and dynamic Islamic welfare state' rather than a theocratic state. The recurring question is whether a state defined by religion can forge a democratic consensus[20]. That question has also arisen in Afghanistan after Karzai's appointment as President on 7 December 2004. Meanwhile, Washington's anti-terrorist strategy will continue to be endangered by the lack of political consensus and the prevalence of support for extremism among sections of Pakistan's army, intelligence services and political parties. In the elections of 2002 the Muttahida Majlis-e-Amal (MMA, the United Action Front) emerged as the third largest group in parliament and won a majority in the NWFP. The MMA included the Jamiat-e-Ulema-e-Islam which was linked to the Taliban and the extremist Jamiat-e-Islami. The strong showing of the MMA, a coalition of radical Islamic parties, in the NWFP may have reflected the annoyance of Pakistani Pashtuns at Musharraf's support to the US against the Taliban regime, which was dominated by Afghan Pashtuns.[21] But the MMA, which has been part of the ruling coalition since the elections of October 2002, was not an obstacle against terrorism in the border areas. Whether Musharraf's overtures, on 24 November 2004, to Benazir Bhutto and Nawaz Sharif, both of whom were barred from contesting elections, were intended to give a fillip simultaneously to the anti-terrorist campaign and to more democratic forces, was uncertain.

Pakistan's Help against Terrorism: Its Uses as an Ally

US-Pakistan cooperation in the war on terror took place on several fronts. They included coordination of intelligence and law enforcement agencies in hunting Al Qaeda and other terrorists within Pakistan, coordination with military and law enforcement agencies along the border with Afghanistan, and efforts to strengthen Pakistan's law enforcement and counter-terrorism capabilities and institutions. The US and Pakistan had collaborated successfully on counter-narcotics for more than a decade, especially in the tribal areas near the Afghan border.

After 9/11, Musharraf, like most heads of state, was quick to express sympathy with the US and oppose terrorists. Musharraf juggled with several balls in the air and played on different levels. As the US announced that it would overthrow the Taliban government, he offered military facilities. Assuring Washington that Pakistan would side with the US against a Muslim country carried its domestic risks. He persuaded Washington of his anti-terrorist convictions by banning some terrorist organisations. At the same time Pakistan continued to connive in the organisation of terrorist attacks in Kashmir.

It was evident that whatever Musharraf's government was doing against terrorism, it had a hand in the training of terrorists who crossed over the Line of Control into Jammu & Kashmir. After the attacks in December 2001 and June and December 2002 on Kashmir, Musharraf promised to end infiltrations across the border[22], implicitly acknowledging that Pakistan had been behind them. On 21 February 2002, Daniel Pearl, a reporter with the *Wall Street Journal*, was killed. Then, on 8 May, Al Qaeda carried out an attack on the Sheraton Hotel in Karachi. Pakistan announced a new anti-terrorist initiative on 13 May, but on 14 June the Harakat-ul-Mujahideen bombed the US consulate in Karachi. One of its members, captured in July 2004, admitted that they had tried to kill Musharraf. Terrorist attacks took place in Kashmir in September and December 2002.

Even as terrorist attacks continued, militants were arrested, Lashkar-e-Taiba outlawed and the offices and bank accounts of several terrorist organisations closed down. More than 2000 suspected militants were arrested. Musharraf also replaced some of the top officers in the intelligence services and claimed that the organisation's ties to militants in Afghanistan and Kashmir had been cut off. Pakistan tried and convicted the four people involved in the plot against Daniel Pearl. The Bush administration was convinced that Musharraf was a moderate politician, fighting terrorists and seeking to improve relations with India. Pakistan was an ally of the US in the campaign against terrorism. It had handed over more than 500 Al Qaeda suspects to the Americans since 9/11. The campaign was stepped up between June and September 2004. Musharraf boasted in September 2004 that Pakistan was the main contributor to the campaign against terror. However, some commentators saw the campaign as the result of American pressure rather than Musharraf's wish to stem the tide of terrorism[23].

The second was finding bin Laden and hunting down members of the Taliban and Al Qaeda. On 27 October 2001, Pakistan announced that it had handed over a suspected Al Qaeda member, Said of Yemen, who was allegedly responsible for the attack on USS 'Cole' in Aden in 2000. Musharraf also pressed the Taliban government to hand over bin Laden to the US. On 8 November 2001, Musharraf announced that Pakistan had started searching for bin Laden; less than three weeks later he said that bin Laden was not in Pakistan. Pakistan forbade the Afghan ambassador in Islamabad to hold a press conference and ordered the closure of the Afghan consulates in Peshawar and Quetta[24].

In September 2004 Musharraf himself put the onus for waging a successful war against terrorism on the West, in particular, on the US. Visiting New York in September

2004, Musharraf referred to the need to address the underlying causes of terrorism. He linked this to his concern about an iron curtain descending between Islam and the West. Terrorism reflected disaffection and frustration in the Islamic world. He did not mention Palestine and Kashmir. The West, he said, should give financial aid for an Islamic renaissance. Then, on 6 December, he averred that terrorism was caused by political disputes – implying Palestine and Kashmir – and economic problems. These statements may have been partly an answer to his domestic critics, partly an attempt to enhance his international image as a spokesman for Muslims. His saying that the US was wrong to wage war against Iraq and that it would not win the war against terrorism may have reflected his dismay or annoyance at the Bush administration's refusal to give Pakistan F-16 fighter aircraft[25]. Probably it also mirrored his domestic weakness: his reiteration of Pakistan's traditional policy of mentioning Kashmir as a cause of terrorism could not have been calculated to please India. To that extent it would not strengthen the anti-terrorist front between India, Pakistan and the US.

The third strand in the anti-terrorist campaign was to pursue militants in the areas bordering Afghanistan[26]. They included the North-West Frontier Province, Southern Waziristan and Baluchistan. On several occasions, bin Laden was reported to be in hiding in the region. Traditionally these areas were regarded as a no-man's land, as among the most dangerous places in the world, and had never been under central control. Islam had never united the feuding tribes of Pakistan, and the centre had bought them off with jobs and non-interference. After 1947 the tribes were left to govern themselves, and under a system of patronage, did not create too many problems for the state. Pakistani governments remained on amicable terms with the tribes through a system of subsidies while protecting them from Afghanistan. Tribal *jirgas* dispensed justice and defied the idea of one law for the whole country. The Pashtuns are among the poorest people of Pakistan, and politically and socially marginalised.

The border areas are economically important, because of vast gas reserves in Baluchistan. But the province, with a population of some eight million, is one of Pakistan's poorest areas and it is doubtful that Pakistan can guarantee security for a new trans Iran-Pakistan-India pipeline. The appointment of Zafrullah Khan Jamali, a Baluch, as prime minister on 21 November 2002, was intended to assuage the feelings of the Baluch tribesmen who felt their welfare had been ignored by a series of governments in Islamabad. The tribes wanted not just jobs but greater powers for the regional government. Islamabad is concerned that unrest in Baluchistan could trigger rebellion by other tribes, including the Pashtuns.

So when the Pakistani army, along with American forces, deployed 70,000 troops on the Afghan-Pakistani border, it met with resistance. About 25,000 troops were stationed in the tribal areas. The campaign of Pakistani and American troops was entirely punitive and threatened to alienate the tribes. With militants from the Taliban hiding in these areas they could become a hotbed of extremism. There were several clashes between American and Pakistani troops, and between them and local tribesmen, as well as instances of army men being kidnapped by tribesmen.

The October 2002 elections resulted in the MMA winning a majority in the North-West Frontier province. The MMA campaigned on a strong anti-American platform and criticised the US for hunting down terrorists in the province. Some of its luminaries, belonging to the Jamiat-e-Islami and the Jamiat-Ulema-Islami-Fazlur, called for *jihad* against American threats to Pakistan's sovereignty[27]. However, the MMA could not hamper the American pursuits along the Afghan-Pakistani border, for the government of the NWFP had no authority over the Federally Administered Tribal Areas where most Taliban and Al Qaeda fighters were reportedly in hiding. The tribal areas were administered by the centre, and Pakistani forces, not local police, were used to hunt militants. Pakistani and American troops had combined against them, and occasional skirmishes betwen Pakistani and American forces in Waziristan had not stopped the campaign.

The military operations led to the arrest of a handful of Taliban and Al Qaeda members such as Nek Muhammad, as well as the escape of other militants, including the Uzbek Tahir Yuldashev and the Egyptian Ayman Al-Zawari. The Pashtuns regarded the Pakistani operations as an intrusion on their sovereignty, and the 'all sticks' policy closed the door to negotiations. An economic gift to develop the area might have served as a sign of conciliation, but it was not offered. Military force was the order of the day; political reform seemed to have been shelved. Contrary to Pakistani and American claims, the operations against Al Qaeda in December 2004 showed that they were still at large. American officials found that Islamabad lacked the political will to hunt Taliban members linked by ethnicity and family to Pakistani Pashtuns[28]. In February 2004 Musharraf himself admitted that extremists were crossing over from Pakistan to Afghanistan[29].

By 2004 the campaign in the tribal areas was regarded by some as a reflection of Bush's need to win the presidential election in November 2004. Whatever the correctness of this view it reflects the scepticism about the motives behind the anti-tribal military operations. In November Pakistan announced measures to conciliate the tribes. Pakistan would remove all checkpoints set up during recent army operations against Al Qaeda militants in the tribal areas bordering Afghanistan. Innocent tribesmen arrested during operations would be freed. Islamabad hoped that these concessions would boost support from tribesmen, some of whom promised not to support the hundreds of Al Qaeda militants hiding in the area. How the tribal areas will be monitored after the dismantling of the checkposts is unclear[30].

More generally, Washington is concerned that the Taliban and Al Qaeda continue to receive weapons and training from Pakistan, and that the rank and file of Pakistan's security forces are ill-disposed towards the US[31]. On the whole, then, it appears that under American pressure, Islamabad has tried to assert its authority in the tribal areas, but without much success.

Terrorism and Democracy in Pakistan

The military offensive against terrorism, combined with the American emphasis on fighting for freedom, does draw attention to the problems of containing extremism within Pakistan and the prospects of democratisation there. Pakistan's commitment to democracy and human rights would be central to building a stable, positive future for its people. So, in April 2002, the Bush administration welcomed the referendum conducted by Musharraf to legitimise his rule and advised him to hold national elections.

These elections, held in October 2002, although flawed, restored a prime minister, a National Assembly and four provincial assemblies. Pakistan's parliament began to function, and a devolution programme, American officials claimed, was revitalising local government. American democracy programmes were assisting the development of accountable, responsive democratic institutions and practices, including effective legislatures and local councils that responded to citizens, and that played a positive role in governance. The US also supported much needed political party reform, the development of an independent media that would provide balanced information and effective civil society advocacy. Educators, the media, and civil society leaders, as well as younger, non-elite Pakistanis in communities resistant to democratic values were all being engaged in the debates on political liberalisation in Pakistan.

A USAID programme was re-established to provide Pakistan assistance in education. In March 2004, Powell announced the Bush administration's intention to confer major non-NATO ally status on Pakistan. The US and Pakistan would discuss ways of expanding 'our close, long-term partnership' in a number of areas: cooperation against terrorism, economic exchanges and regional consultations. This decision underscored the continuing importance of Pakistan's role in the American-led front against international terrorism, particularly in the continuing fight against Al Qaeda and the Taliban.

Washington was convinced that, after a prolonged impasse, democracy was gaining ground in Pakistan. Once again, the Bush administration drew attention to Pakistan's role in pursing terrorists in its border areas. Equally important was American encouragement to Islamabad to build good, constructive relations with Afghanistan and to support Karzai's efforts to establish a stable and secure government. Pakistan was also being helped to strengthen non-proliferation export controls.

In the coming years, the US and Pakistan would strengthen bilateral cooperation in order to deal successfully with issues of mutual interest, including counter-terrorism, Pakistan's ties with its neighbours, regional stability, the strengthening of Pakistan's democracy, economic development, and the enhancement of the life chances of its people. Together with support for the development of the independent media and effective civil society advocates, these measures would help Pakistan to develop into a stable, moderate Islamic state.

Democracy in Pakistan

Washington regarded a return to full democracy in Pakistan as central to long-term stability. There were two main reasons for this. First, Pakistan's highly centralised government, dominated by the military since the mid-1950s, is an embarrassment to the US which professes to counter terrorism partly by promoting democracy, and with the intent of defending democratic values. So some aid is to be spent on decentralisation and the strengthening of local government.

Secondly, Washington has put pressure on Musharraf to control religious extremists in Pakistan. This was partially linked to a new aid programme to promote educational reform to lessen the influence of extremist ideas in *madrasas*. On the whole, American officials apparently remain convinced of Musharraf's commitment to democracy and human rights. So the Bush administration was not perturbed at Musharraf's decision to remain as army chief till December 2007; the topic did not come up in his talks with Bush in September or December 2004.

The question is how Pakistan can become a democracy[32]. Domestic factors play the primary role in a country's transition to democracy, but can a regional environment or international intervention encourage democratisation? Post-communist Europe shows that such an environment can give some inspiration: the example of Western Europe, peaceful and democratic for more than half a century, inspired and strengthened the resolve of many East Europeans to build democracy in their own countries.

Is Islam the barrier to democracy? This question is prompted by the fact that Pakistan, like most Muslim-majority states, is not a democracy and that its elected governments have been overthrown by the military on several occasions. Pakistan may be described as a state where military and bureaucratic rule have been interrupted by occasional elections[33]. Does this mean that Islam and democracy are incompatible? Not necessarily. Election results in neighbouring India, which has the world's second-largest Muslim population, show that political and religious affiliation are not aligned, either for Muslims or the Hindu majority – or for any religious community.

Is the definition of the state an obstacle to democratisation? If religion in itself is not necessarily a barrier to democracy, one has to probe further to identify barriers to democratisation in Pakistan. The question arises whether Pakistan's definition as a religious state could be a barrier to democracy. Any ideological definition of a state limits intellectual and political choice – whether that ideology is communism, religion or culture. This is because

Pakistan was created as a nation-state, in the literal sense of the alignment of (in this case) the religious nation and territory; as a homeland of Muslims on the Indian subcontinent.

Pakistan's own experience suggests that even elected rulers have had to prove that they are the 'best' Muslims, indeed the Taliban, created by General Zia-ul-Haq, was sustained by the elected government of Benazir Bhutto. The assumption that the religious nation is – or should be – a monolithic whole creates a problem by preventing or restricting the freedom of choice innate in democracy. And, given the lack of legitimacy of military rulers, it is probably a reason why the military struck up an alliance with religious extremists to shore up its legitimacy[34].

In contrast, in India, where Hindus comprise 80 per cent of the population, Hindu nationalists have never won a majority at the centre and are resentful that the Indian state does not identify with the Hindu majority or Hinduism. In India, secularism, implying the separation of church from state, is essential for the acceptance of intellectual and political pluralism, equality of all citizens before the law, and for individual rights against the state.

Religion inspired the creation of Pakistan, but it has not forged a political consensus. Who is to interpret the will of Allah? Is it an unelected general, political/religious moderates or extremists, or 'the people' in a free and fair election? Can the very idea of Pakistan work[35]? Those are the questions currently without answers in Pakistan. Authoritarian states, by their very nature, cannot forge consensus; and the absence of agreement on the rules of governance only reflects the illegitimacy of their rulers.

This explains to some extent why the Pakistani military has nurtured extremism. Since Pakistan's creation was rooted in opposition to India, which has been branded as a permanent enemy, terrorism has become one of the weapons to be used against India. Also, Pakistan inherited, and continued with, an authoritarian tradition from the British. Pakistan's weak politicians were unable to heal sectarian and regional divisions, which made it difficult for them to frame a constitution for a democratic Pakistan. In fact, Ayub Khan's coup took place only two years after the promulgation of Pakistan's first constitution in 1956. Since Pakistan's birth no elected government has ever completed its term in office; and since 1958, all have held office at the pleasure of the army. The military appeared as the only power capable of patching up the country's divisions and introducing better governance, but the reality was more complex. The military acquired control over domestic and foreign policy, the budget, and powers of patronage in both the state and private sectors. The military's determination to sever Jammu & Kashmir from India meant that 6 per cent of Pakistan's GDP was spent on defence. It was also determined to acquire weapons of mass destruction. All these factors, combined with the military's wish to acquire legitimacy, encouraged it to foster extremist groups. To embarrass India, Pakistan backed insurgencies in the Punjab and Jammu Kashmir, and the image of India as the eternal foe led the military to conceive of, and practise, war and terrorism to weaken and defeat India.

The military's belief that *jihads* were needed to fight in Jammu & Kashmir resulted in the education and training of terrorists. The world-view of the terrorists was not confined to India – or even India and Afghanistan. It included the US and Israel[36]. Islamic militants, trained by Pakistan's intelligence and army, have the capability and wish to attack American interests. Since 9/11, because of Musharraf's support to the US, he and those believed to be close to him in the military have been perceived as threats to Islam and targets for assassination. Because of the perception of India as the threat to Pakistan the military and intelligence will not give up their association with terrorists.

Musharraf watered down the policies that had fostered religious extremism domestically and internationally. Pakistan gave bases to the US in the anti-Taliban war and appeared to clamp down on extremist organisations. But it was difficult for the military – as a whole – to sever all ties with its extremist allies partly out of habit or inclination, partly because former allies could be transformed into dangerous enemies of the state, partly because lack of knowledge about their popular reach made it impolitic to break with them. Neither military nor elected governments had the intent or the will to set Pakistan on the course of intellectual and political pluralism.

Moderating the *Madrasas*

Madrasas – religious schools – have been a provenance of extremism in Pakistan. The *madrasas* are difficult to deal with[37]. The failure of Pakistani governments to set up a national educational system has left *madrasas* as the only form of schooling for an estimated one-third of all Pakistani children or almost two million. People go to *madrasas* because of the lack of better educational facilities. Originally intended as centres for Islamic theology, they have instead taught their students the theory and practice of extremism; they trained Taliban and Al Qaeda fighters, and many of those involved in Shia-Sunni violence. Some of the Pakistani intelligence officers were recruited from *madrasas* in the early 1990s. In a society in which more than half the population remains illiterate and facilities for civic education are scarce, *madrasas* are an important source of education, political and social ideas, grounded in extremist versions of Islam. Many a *jihadi* has been trained in a *madrasa*. The Taliban leadership learned their brand of Islam in *madrasas* financed by Saudi Arabia and by extremist parties linked to the Taliban, including the Jamiat-e-Ulema Islam. At least 10 to 15 per cent of the *madrasas* promoted an extremist form of Islam. As many as two-thirds of *madrasas* are run by Deobandis who are hostile to the Shias and connected to the Sipah-e-Sahiba terrorist group.

In 2002 Musharraf, like his predecessors, affirmed that *madrasas* would be integrated into the main education sector. He also declared his intent to reform the *madrasas* as part of his government's anti-terrorist campaign in accordance with UNSC Resolution 1373. But no decisive action has been taken to date; no time frame set to reform the system. The Deeni Madaris Ordinance intervention in the *madrasa* system suggested that *madrasas* would submit to intervention voluntarily; there were no enforcement measures. New textbooks, teaching more moderate versions of Islam were offered,[38] but these were half-hearted measures, intended to assuage Washington. The political calculation was probably that leaving the *madrasas* alone would avert confrontation between the clergy and military. The military are threatened by them, but need the clergys' support for their anti-India stance.

For the US education 'is an asset crucial to Pakistan's development as a moderate Muslim nation'[39]. The 9/11 Commission Report proposed 'comprehensive' American support to reform Pakistan's educational system. Congress endorsed this suggestion in the FY 2005 Appropriations Bill and asked the Secretary of State to improve secular education and develop a moderate curriculum for primary schools in Pakistan[40]. The US gave financial aid to Pakistan to change its educational system, especially the syllabi of *madrasas*. But this intervention to reform *madrasas* could not alter certain realities of Pakistani politics and society. Secular education cannot be promoted by a state which is defined by religion, and which uses religion to mobilise political support. So it is imprudent – perhaps impossible – for Musharraf to change horses in mid-stream, by introducing new syllabi in the many *madrasas* having teachers with extremist inclinations. In June 2004, Musharraf himself admitted that many *madrasas'* are involved in militancy and extremism'[41].

Even in the moderate schools students are taught that Pakistan is besieged by aggressors; that there is a Jewish-Hindu plot to dominate the world. Anti-American and anti-Shia teaching is common. Consequently, many Pakistanis believe that their enemies are blocking the glorious renaissance of Islam and their country's greatness. Even Musharraf is perceived as an 'agent' of Pakistan's foes[42].

American funding for educational change in Pakistan has been 'a drop in the bucket'[43]. Terrorism and the absence of democracy in Pakistan illustrate the impact of extremist thinking on Pakistani politics and society, and how they could work against the attainment of the American goal of defeating terrorism.

The elections of 2002 did little to produce a sustained transition to democracy[44]. An EU observer group received no guarantee on the safety of its members who were to oversee the elections. Shortly before the elections, on 21 August, Musharraf announced the Legal Framework Order, which undermined democratic institutions and reinforced the powers of the military. The Order provided for a National Security Council, which is dominated by unelected members having the power to decide the fate of the elected representatives. The Bush government supported him after the introduction of the Legal Framework Order, although it realised that the Order could hamper the building of strong democratic institutions[45].

The Bush administration put pressure on Musharraf to create the National Security Council through a legislative process in April 2004. He browbeat Jamali to push a bill through parliament. That did nothing to change the spirit of Pakistani politics. The military's political pre-eminence was consolidated: it could monitor the activities of elected members of the National Assembly and could veto any decision taken by it. This was Musharraf's idea of 'checks and balances.' In 2003 parliament passed a single piece of legislation – the budget. Amendments to the constitution would need the military's approval. Musharraf presented himself with a five-year presidential term and powers to decide when the Senate, National and Provincial Assemblies would meet. He had the power to make changes to the constitution even after the new parliament came into existence. Musharraf has unlimited power to amend the constitution, appoint judges and chiefs of staff. Through the National Security Council he can dismiss the prime minister, which he did in June 2004, when he replaced Jamali with Shaukat Aziz, and also the national and regional legislatures. If a politically inconvenient party wins a majority in a provincial election, he can nullify the election by dissolving the provincial assembly through the National Security

Council. Musharraf also gave himself the power to appoint governments without consulting the prime minister. He has the authority to appoint an interim government when the assembly is dissolved before elections. He cannot be overruled by any court. He reintroduced the Eighth Amendment, which was imposed on a partyless National Assembly in 1985. Article 58 (2) gave him the power to dissolve the National Assembly. This article was introduced by General Zia-ul-Haq who used it to cut short the tenures of Nawaz Sharif and Benazir Bhutto.

Since assuming power in 1999, Musharraf has claimed that he wants to transform Pakistan into a moderate Muslim nation. But his performance is mixed at best. He is one of the military autocrats, buoyed by the US, since the Cold War. That is part of Pakistan's problem, not its solution. Despite proclaiming his wish to improve the living conditions of Pakistanis, so that they are not tempted to become militant Islamists, Musharraf spends most of the aid on buying arms. But are fighter aircraft the best way to eradicate terrorists? If, as he himself says, the real threat to Pakistan comes from terrorists within the country, they would best be countered by a combination of higher economic spending and political liberalisation.

The larger problem in Pakistan stems from the existence of multiple layers of government and fanciful strategic notions. Different branches of government and different groups outside the government make and carry out their own policies which they consider to be in the national interest of their 'Islamic' state. Indeed that is why they have trained militants and will probably continue to do so.

Just as US economic and military largesse has strengthened the military regime, Musharraf's inability to practise inclusive politics, and the absence of political forces opposed to Islamic militancy, have emboldened and empowered Pakistan's *jihadis*. Musharraf has professed the politics of moderation but there are few signs that this is the practice of Pakistani politics. Perhaps this is because even the 'moderation' – whatever that means – is constricted by the ideology of the religious nation-state and makes excuses for the existence of terrorism – at least against India. But it is precisely those excuses, borne out of political expediency, that could harm American interests in South Asia. Parliament's confirmation of Musharraf in his dual role as army chief until 2007 will not change very much. America's backing for Musharraf avoids inconvenient questions and facts about him and Pakistan.

What is the Significance of US Economic Aid to Pakistan?

The Bush administration claimed that the alliance with Pakistan had facilitated the capture of Al Qaeda and Taliban remnants and the removal of the root causes of terrorism by providing substantial amounts for macroeconomic stabilisation and growth, and support for social sector programmes. Pakistan's programmes for structural macroeconomic management had impressed the international donor community. USAID had supported grassroots economic development and health programmes visible to ordinary Pakistanis. The US had also urged Musharraf to introduce educational reforms which would help prepare young Pakistanis to gain employment and compete in the global marketplace. It gave financial aid to reform *madrasas* so that they ceased to be breeding centres of terrorism.

The anti-terrorist coalition resulted in largesse

American to Pakistan. With the promise of a multi-year $3 billion US aid package, General Musharraf, like his predecessors, thinks he has a *carte blanche* to consolidate military rule. The aid has been given unconditionally: the US has waived democracy-related sanctions against Pakistan, promised $600 million in annual aid for the next five years and helped Pakistan secure $1.7 billion each year from international financial institutions. But it is unlikely that economic aid in itself is enough either to bolster a dictator or to encourage him to democratise. Given Pakistan's military-dominated, over-centralised political system, could or should more aid be given to local development programmes that seek to promote decentralisation, local participation, accountability and enhance good governance? Even if Pakistan retains its 'Islamic' definition and remains in a perpetual 'grey zone' between dictatorship and democratisation, at least the principles of moderation could be encouraged. But the signs are that aid for local administration, health treatment, education and political parties is inadequate to balance the dominance of the military: indeed this aid may be reinforcing over-centralisation. And most of the largesse continues to be spent on stockpiling weapons. Washington may be deluding itself, not for the first time, that high growth rates will engineer political stability in Pakistan.

Every dictator – Field Marshal Ayub Khan, between 1958-69, General Yahya Khan, who seemed 'perennially' to be introducing a phased return to democracy between 1969 and 1971, and General Zia-ul-Haq, who claimed to build a 'true Islamic state' – of his definition – between 1977 and 1988, used the Kashmir dispute to justify high defence expenditure. This only facilitated the spread of radical Islamic ideas in the army, making it home to religious hardliners. Probably because it shores up the military, Washington has never said or done anything to dispel these beliefs. It suspended military supplies to both India and Pakistan. For his part, General Yahya Khan thought that the US would help him to stabilise Pakistan domestically and help it to wrest Kashmir from India. He was disappointed. All the dictators assumed that the US would 'save' them. General Yahye Khan thought the Nixon administration would prevent the secession of East Pakistan; Zia-ul-Haq did not foresee a Soviet retreat from Afghanistan (admittedly he was not the only one) and the decline of American interest in Pakistan soon thereafter. Like his predecessors, Musharraf seems to look on American support as an insurance policy for his political survival, which in turn is indispensable for Pakistan's progress.

Unconditional American aid is only reinforcing military domination of Pakistan and giving Musharraf the mistaken impression that he can do what he likes. The US would benefit by holding his regime accountable for its conflicting policies. So would Pakistan, whose military rulers have chosen to believe that American aid will press India into settling the Kashmir dispute on Pakistan's terms. The military's continuing reliance on the clergy only highlights these illusions; did the Indo-US deals of March 2006 dispel them?

Is Musharraf committed to rooting out terrorism in Pakistan? Since he himself has been the target of militant attacks it is reasonable to assume that he is. On the other hand, he seems unable or unwilling to eliminate Taliban supporters from the army and intelligence services, and is prone to justify militant activities in Jammu & Kashmir as those of 'indigenous insurgents' rather than terrorists. Once again, he is bound by the religious definition of the Pakistani state. But Washington persists in hailing Musharraf as the man who will steer Pakistan towards democracy.

As in the case of post-communist Europe a decade ago, democracy and regional security are linked in 'post-Taliban' Asia; the fight against terrorism gives democracy promotion an international dimension. The extent to which the US can influence Islamabad into reining extremist elements in and so containing the terrorist challenge to international peace and security may remain limited.

Defined by religion, having a predominantly Muslim population, yet lacking consensus, Pakistan, under American pressure, has supported the US against the Taliban and Al Qaeda. Perhaps it might be more correct to say that its support is only partial, for it remains an exporter of Islamic militancy: it shows how a weak state can become an exporter of instability. For the US, Pakistan is a frontline state against terrorism, but the absence of consensus makes it unstable. Apparently Washington shies away from facing this awkward reality. Musharraf is distancing himself from extremist elements – if only because they threaten his very existence. Religious violence has almost doubled in Pakistan since 2001. Under American pressure, Asaf Zardari (Benazir Bhutto's husband) and Nawaz Sharif were released on November 2004[46], but the crucial question is whether all parties will observe the rules of the democratic game. Authoritarianism cannot win the war against terrorism, but will greater political liberalisation accomplish that?

Is the US caught in a bind? The Bush administration sees Musharraf as its best bet against terrorism, but terrorism will not go away without structural changes in Pakistan's political system[47]. Those changes imply political liberalisation. The military's political paramountcy has only been entrenched by American munificence: that trend will continue as the Bush government presents more *matériel* to Musharraf's government in the name of fighting terrorism. Pakistan's methods of achieving security by using *jihadists* in Jammu & Kashmir have come to threaten the US, Musharraf – and Pakistan itself. And the danger is that nuclear weapons could fall into the hands of extremists.

There is considerable anti-American sentiment in Pakistan. Two-thirds of Pakistanis favour the fusion of religion and politics[48]. About 45 per cent of Pakistanis had confidence in bin Laden's ability 'to do the right thing' in international affairs, and half thought the US was bent upon world domination[49]. A leading American scholar, testifying before the Senate Foreign Relations Committee viewed Pakistan as 'probably the most anti-American country in the world ... ranging from the radical Islamists on one side to the liberals and Westernised elites on the other'[50]. The attempts on Musharraf's life were widely regarded as the handiwork of extremists angered by his turning against the Taliban[51]. Although Musharraf is threatened by extremists, his exclusion of the moderates may only have strengthened radical parties like the MMA.

The situation in Pakistan is complex. Public opinion is against the US. Weak and fragmented political parties have enhanced Musharraf's appeal. Democracy is probably not in great demand in Pakistan, or the extent of that demand is unknown. Musharraf recognises the extremist threat but cannot bring himself to dispense with militants in politics. Religion, anti-Indianism and anti-Americanism are integral components of Pakistani nationalism. The short-term pressures of acquiring military bases against the Taliban shaped the American strategy of giving the Musharraf regime sophisticated weapons; that strategy could work against Washington's long-term aim of defeating terrorism.

References

1. Entry for 19 September 2001, USGCAT 2001; see also Chapter 3, and Husain Haqqani, 'America's New Alliance with Pakistan: Avoiding the Traps of the Past', http://www.ceip.org/files/pdf/Policybrief19.pdf.

2. Entry for 29 October 2001, USGCAT 2001.

3. *Hindustan Times,* 24 November 2004.

4. Entries for 4, 16 October, and 11 November 2001, USGCAT 2001.

5. See my *The Limits of British Influence: South Asia and the Anglo-American Relationship 1947-56* (London and New York 1993), pp. 111-56.

6. State Department Bureau of South Asian Affairs Note on Pakistan, March 2000, www.state.gov/r/pa/ei/bgn/3453.htm.

7. Statement by Christine Rocca, State Department Washington File, 26 March 2003.

8. See my *The Origins of the Partition of India, 1936-1947* (Oxford South Asian Studies Series 1987, 1989, paperback, 1990, 1992, 1995, 1997, 1999. Also published in a special omnibus on the partition of India by Oxford University Press in 2002).

9. See my 'Pakistan's Dangerous Nation-State Ideal: Democratic Pluralism is the Only Cure for Pakistan's Ills', *Asian Wall Street Journal,* 11 October 2001.

10. http://www.un.org/Docs/sc/committees/1267/1267ListEng.htm.

11. State Department, *Patterns of Global Terrorism 2002,* 30 April 2003 and 'Pakistan Asked to Explain Islamic Party Link to Al Qaeda Suspects', Agence France-Presse, 3 March 3003.

12. *Dawn,* 24 November 2003.

13. National Commission on Terrorist Attacks Upon the United States, *The 9/11 Commission Report* (Washington DC Government Printing Office, 2004), p. 309.

14. Husain Haqqani, 'Extremist Groups Review Activities in Pakistan', *The Washington Post*, 9 February 2003.

15. Ibid.

16. 'Three Years of Progress in the War on Terror', State Department Fact Sheet, 11 September 2004, http://www.state.gov/s/ct/rls/fs/2004/36156.htm.

17. Ibid.

18. Ibid.

19. Ashley Tellis, 'US Strategy: Assisting Pakistan's Transformation', *The Washington Quarterly*, Vol. 28, No. 1, p.108.

20. See my 'Only Game in Town', *The World Today*, July 2003, and 'Pakistan's Dangerous Nation-State Ideal,' *Asian Wall Street Journal*, 11 October 2001.

21. 'Pak Islamists Reject US Help in Terror Hunt', *The Times of India*, 26 November 2002.

22. *Dawn*, 12 January 2002.

23. See for example, *Terrorism in South Asia*, CRS-7; BBC report, 22 September 2004; *Dawn*, 26 November 2004; Husain Haqqani, 'Scepticism Over Crackdown', *The Nation* (Lahore), 19 November 2003, and Najam Sethi, 'Writing on the Wall', *The Friday Times* (Lahore), 21 November 2003.

24. Entries for 8 and 21 November 2001, USGCAT 2001.

25. *Dawn*, 8 December 2004.

26. This section is based on Ayesha Khan, 'High Stakes on the Frontier', *The World Today*, October 2004, pp. 19-20; BBC and reports. *Dawn*, 'Threats and Responses: Pakistan Frontier', *The New York Times*, 28 January 2003.

27. For example, 'US Trying to Destabilise Pakistan, Iran: MMA', *Dawn*, 4 November 2003; 'MMA Opposes Pak-US Military Drive', *News* (Karachi), 24 June 2003.

28. Testimony of American army officers before Senate Foreign Relations Committee, cited in *Terrorism in South Asia*, CRS-12.

29. 'Pakistan Says That Afghan Rebels May be Using its Soil', Reuter report, 12 February 2004, cited in ibid.

30. http://news.bbc.co.uk/go/pr/fr/-/2/hi/south_asia/4045457.stm

31. Armitage: 'Some Pakistanis Reluctant to Work With US', Reuter

report, 30 September 2003, cited in 'Terrorism in South Asia', CRS-10.

32. See my 'Only Game in Town', *World Today,* July 2003.

33. Samuel Huntington, *The Third Wave: Democratisation in the Late Twentieth Century* (Norman: University of Oklahoma University Press 1991), p. 308. See also the articles by Alfred Stepan and Graeme Robertson, 'Arab, not Muslim, Exceptionalism', *Journal of Democracy,* Vol. 15, No. 4, 2004, pp. 140-46, and Sanfor Lankoff, 'The Reality of Muslim Exceptionalism', ibid., pp. 133-9.

34. Aqil Shah, 'Democracy On Hold in Pakistan', *Journal of Democracy,* Vol. 13, No. 1, January 2002, pp. 69-75.

35. For a recent discussion, see Stephen P: Cohen, *The Idea of Pakistan* (Washington DC: Brookings Institution, 2004).

36. Tellis, 'Assisting Pakistan', p. 106.

37. P.W.Singer, 'Pakistan's Madrasas: Ensuring a System of Education not Jihad', Analysis paper #14, Brookings Institution, November 2001, and 'Pakistan: Madrasas, Extremism and the Military', International Crisis Group Asia Report no. 36, 29 July 2002; Pakistan: Madrasas, Extremism and the Military, International Crisis Group Asia Report no. 49, 2003. See also Jessica Stern, 'Pakistan's Jihad Culture', *Foreign Affairs,* vol. 79, no. 6, 2000, 115-26.

38. CRS 8.

39. State Department Washington File, 2 March 2004.

40. 'Education in Pakistan', CRS-2.

41. Pervez Musharraf, 'A Plea for Enlightened Moderation', *The Washington Post,* 1 June 2004.

42. International Crisis Group Report, 7 October 2004, 'Pakistan: Reform in the Education Sector'.

43. Lee Hamilton, Vice-Chairman, before the House International Relations Committee on 9/11 Commission Report, cited in 'Education in Pakistan', CRS-4.

44. Sunil Dasgupta, 'Civil-military Relations and Democratisation in Pakistan', *The Friday Times,* 21 December 2001, Husain Haqqani, Gen. Musharraf Can't Lose, Voters Can't Win', *Wall Street Journal,* 10 October 2002, 'They Have No Choice But To Coexist', *Dawn,* 13 October 2002, 'Pakistani Cabinet Take Oath', *The Muslim News,* 24 November 2002, BBC, 23 February 2003, 24 February 2004.

45. State Department Washington File, 22 August 2002.

46. Vikram Sood, 'Why the General is Talking to the Democrats', *Hindustan Times,* 24 November 2004.

47. Walter Andersen, 'South Asia: A Selective War on Terrorism', in Ashley Tellis and Michael Wills (eds), *Strategic Asia, 2005-05: Confronting Terrorism in the Pursuit of Power* (Seattle: National Bureau of Asian Research, 2004), pp. 227-59.

48. International Foundation for Electoral Systems, 'National Public Opinion Survey Pakistan 2004', http://www.plsc.org.pk/survey/index.html.

49. See among others John Lancaster, 'Pakistan Struggles to Put Army on Moderate Course', *The Washington Post,* 4 April 2004; Statement of Stephen Cohen Before the Senate Foreign Relations Committee, 28 January 2004; and Zafar Abbas, 'Musharraf and the Mullahs', BBC report, 30 December 2003.

50. Ibid.

51. 'Musharraf and the Mullahs', BBC report, 30 December 2003.

Chapter 3

The United States and India: Neighbours After 9/11?

Cooperation against terrorism after 9/11 brought about a fundamental transformation in the Indo-US relationship. In November 2001 President Bush and Prime Minister Vajpayee agreed that terrorism threatened the security of the US and India, and also freedom, democracy and security throughout the world. Less than five years later, in March 2006, the US stunned the world by allowing India, which has not signed the Nuclear Non-Proliferation Treaty, into the nuclear club. For its part, India agreed to open its civilian nuclear plants to international inspection. Bush declared that India and the US had put the Cold War behind and moved forward as strategic partners[2].

The agreements signed between Washington and New Delhi on 2 March marked the Bush administration's awareness that the US was not omnipotent, and that it saw India, along with the European Union, Russia, Japan and China, as one of the powers that would help maintain the global balance of power in the twenty-first century. India was upgraded to partnership status, symbolizing the radical change which took off in the wake of India's support for America's anti-Taliban war in 2001. In a joint statement, Bush and Manmohan Singh envisaged that the 'successful transformation of the US-India relationship' would have 'a decisive and positive influence on the future international system' in the twenty-first century. Cooperation against terrorism would continue[3].

It has not always been that way, although India and the US have been the world's largest democracies since the end of the Cold War. However, their relationship during the Cold War was often fractious, partly because Indian non-alignment ruled out military alliances at a time when the Americans, inspired by former Secretary of State John Foster Dulles, classified countries as being with or against the US; partly because South Asia was a low strategic priority for Washington. India was 'not even a blip on the White House radar screen[4]'. And the American insistence that India should 'get on the democratic side immediately[5]' irritated New Delhi. As Raghavan Pillai, the Indian Foreign Secretary in 1954, explained:

> The Soviets have never claimed that they represent the free world and have never asked India ... to join forces with them ... so long as they do not force their views on us, we do not force our views on them. But the case of the free world is different. It is claimed that by refusing to line up with the free world we are doing something morally reprehensible and politically bad. It therefore becomes important for us to know what the free world represents. Such a question does not arise with regard to the Soviet Union, as we know what Communism means [before and after independence] and have been fighting it even while others were fraternising with Moscow [during the Second World War][6].

India's non-alignment was perceived by the US as weak-kneed, and the political friction between them lasted throughout the Cold War. To India, non-alignment represented the maximising of diplomatic options – a normal tenet of any country's foreign policy. The US, however, thought India was trying to choose between the West and the Soviet Union, and found it hard to accept that India merely wished to judge issues on their merits, and that included criticising American policy when it saw fit to do so[7]. The fact that the US was India's largest aid donor did nothing to lessen the misunderstanding between them.

At the end of the Cold War, the US was left as the only superpower. Non-alignment lost the connotations it had had, as a force between, or as an alternative to, the Western and communist blocs, during the Cold War. With the disintegration of the USSR, India lost its main arms supplier and trading partner, and, like all countries, had to redefine its international relationships[8]. India had to search for a new role in a world dominated by the lone superpower, one in which military alliances seemingly receded into the background, and the economic strength of countries accounted relatively more for their world standing. In the 1950s, India and many East Asian countries were economically on a par with one another; India was perceived by the West as the only political and economic counterpoise to Communist China and as a potentially great Asian power. At the beginning of the twenty-first century, that potential is yet to be realised. Many East Asian countries have surpassed India economically, and Japan is a member of the G-8. It has been argued that India's development from the grassroots may sustain economic development better than that of China[9] – but that prospect lies in the future. India's understandable preoccupation with its own problems, and the fact that Nehru's successors have lacked his international stature, have restricted India's role on the world stage. But especially after 9/11, India's economic promise and the resilience of its democracy are recognised by the US as significant contributors to Asian security in the new millennium. Economically the US has welcomed the liberalisation of the Indian economy and wants India to open its markets to more American goods. India had a trade surplus with the US in agricultural goods in 2002. American exports to India were between $3.5 and 4 billion after 1997; US investment in India fell from $737 million in 1997 to a mere $283 million in 2002.

The US and India had a mutual interest in improving their relations in the post-Cold War world. Prime Minister Narasimha Rao's official visit to the US in 1994 marked the first attempt to end the discord that had characterised the 'cold peace' between Washington and New Delhi. Both countries sought to increase trading ties and to sort out differences on nuclear non-proliferation.

The US is appreciative of India's economic progress, its development in the area of information technology and software. Any differences between their governments are on a different plane from the friendly personal ties between individual Indians and Americans. India is the world's largest exporter of students to the US: there were more than 80,000 in 2004-05 and the numbers rose despite more stringent American immigration rules after 9/11[10].

In the 1980s American administrations fretted about India as a nuclear problem of the first magnitude, because of its refusal to sign the nuclear non-proliferation treaty. This issue dominated Indo-US exchanges. India resented what it saw as American lectures on what Washington thought should be in its national interest. India was not seen as a partner in solving major international problems; rather it was regarded as a nuclear power threatening nuclear proliferation. India and the US engaged in a dialogue of the deaf that did not bring them closer on nuclear issues[11]. India's nuclear test in 1998 led the US to impose sanctions. Talks between Jaswant Singh and Strobe

Talbott foundered because India refused to sign the Comprehensive Test Ban Treaty (CTBT).

Bill Clinton's visit to India in March 2000, the first by an American president in two decades, marked a turning point in Indo-US relations. Clinton and Prime Minister Vajpayee discussed the expansion of economic links, regional stability, environmental and nuclear issues, and security and counter-terrorism. Dialogue between the two countries was institutionalised through the formation of new working groups and the signing of agreements on a gamut of issues. After coming to power in January 2001, President George Bush continued to mend fences with New Delhi and integrated India into American strategic doctrine. Sanctions were lifted without reference to the CTBT. In response, India endorsed Bush's national missile defence programme on 1 May 2001.

The US saw the relationship going from strength to strength after 9/11 in spirit and in substance. India was the first country to offer the US military bases to strike against the Taliban regime. This unprecedented offer marked a sea change in their relationship. India supported the American intervention in Afghanistan, which was legitimised by the UN. As Jaswant Singh, then Minister of Defence put it, 'If one of the instruments of terrorism is military – and the whole point of spreading terror is through military or causing military means. How can you respond to a strike of steel by any other means than steel?' Unlike Pakistan, India never recognised the Taliban government, which it equated with terrorism and regarded as a surrogate for Al Qaeda[12].

India recognised the government of Muhammad Rabbani, leader of the Northern Alliance. So, at the Bonn

Conference in December 2001, Indian diplomacy was instrumental in persuading some members of the Northern Alliance to accept the new realities of power in Afghanistan[13].

The US and India would appear to be natural partners in a campaign against global terrorism. Both agree that the eradication of terrorism is essential for stability in South Asia. Since the 1980s, India had faced its own problems with Sikh and Muslim militants in Punjab and Kashmir, respectively. India had long held that those militants had global networks and was chagrined and indignant at American indifference to its complaints. So India was quick to express sympathy with the US. For its part, the US recognised that Indians had confronted terrorism at home for more than a decade, and that the international nexus of terrorists made it impossible for a terrorist attack on one country to be isolated from a terrorist attack on another. Both India and the US wanted terrorists to be brought to justice. Fighting terrorism was a matter of survival for their citizens and for their shared democratic values. In the words of Robert Blackwill, then American Ambassador in New Delhi, 'We must get the terrorists before they get us'[14].

What changed qualitatively after 9/11? The greatest transformation took place in military cooperation. 'Interoperability' sums up the new relationship in which the US and India share strategic doctrines and operations to face the challenge of terrorism – and more generally, security problems in the twenty-first century[15]. This is explained by the US in terms of the convergence of democratic values, vital national interests and expanding people-to-people ties. India promised the US unconditional help and military facilities against terrorism. During Operation Enduring

Freedom the Indian navy escorted and protected American shipping through the Straits of Malacca. US naval ships were allowed to use Indian ports for rest and refuelling, and India gave the American navy the logistical flexibility it needed to conduct trans-oceanic operations. American air force aircrafts were allowed over-flight, which saved them hundreds of hours[16].

The events of 11 September 2001 opened doors to new forms of strategic cooperation between India and the US. American arms sales went up from negligible amounts in 2001 to $200 million in 2003. The US sold new weapons to India. They included, in 2002, the sale of Firefinder Radar equipment worth more than $200 million, and equipment to counter terrorism. India acquired American anti-missile and electronic warfare systems.

The US authorised Israel to sell to India the American-Israeli Phalcon early warning system, which some believe has tilted the regional strategic balance in India's favour. But the American Defence Department opposed the sale by Israel of the Arrow Weapons System, which was developed by the US. This attitude suggests that there are differences on strategic issues between Washington and New Delhi. In particular, the US may wish to pursue its traditional policy of maintaining a strategic balance in South Asia. This will only annoy India, since that balance can only be preserved by giving Pakistan the arms which it has usually ended up using against India. However, Pakistan is irked at American arms sales to India which it sees strengthening India at its expense. Some see an American tilt towards India since 9/11; Pakistan remains concerned about the US siding with India in the not too distant future.

India and the US both wanted to develop capabilities, jointly address multilateral security issues, including sea-lanes, energy supplies and peace keeping. Their air forces learned about each other's formation flying techniques and practised the coordination of dropping ground support cargo. Links were forged in several aspects of military operations and doctrine. Indian military personnel took part in the international military education and training programmes. The American and Indian armed forces established contact and there were regular exercises and exchanges on terrorism, transnational crime and cyber crime.

Militarily India and the US expanded cooperation in three specific areas – civilian nuclear activities, space programmes and high technology trade. Missile defence, ways to enhance cooperation in the peaceful uses of space technology and nuclear non-proliferation regulations were also discussed. Their navies jointly patrolled the Straits of Malacca. Some of the groups that had carried out terrorist attacks on India were placed on the US foreign terrorist organisation list. Eight alleged members from the Lashkar-e-Taiba group were prosecuted in Virginia and Pennsylvania. Joint Steering Groups between the American and Indian militaries meet regularly. The Defence Policy Group, which seemed to have withered away after India's nuclear test in 1998, was revived in the autumn of 2001.

Since 2002 the Indian and American armed forces have held joint exercises. Some of these gave the US its first chance to look at Russian aircraft sold to India. In September 2003 their armies conducted a joint exercise near the Sino-Indian border, and the 'Malabar 2003' naval exercises included an American nuclear submarine. 'Malabar 2004' followed, off the coast of Goa. In July 2004 the Indian Air Force participated in exercises in Alaska. Earlier, in March, Powell hailed the current relationship between the US and India as 'the best ... that has existed between our two great democracies in many, many years – if not in history'[17].

The US-India Joint Working Group on Counter-terrorism was set up in January 2000. Increased cooperation in containing terrorism is a significant aspect of the Indo-US strategic partnership after 9/11. In May 2002, New Delhi and Washington set up the Indo-US Cyber Security Forum to protect critical infrastructures from cyber attacks. The Bush administration provided India with border security systems and training, and takes the view that India and the US can jointly tackle terrorists in Sri Lanka and Nepal. Regarding India as 'a close ally in the global war against terrorism', the US has continued to increase military cooperation to counter terrorism. In June 2004 the Joint Defence Group underlined more areas of convergence on fundamental values, and Bush and Manmohan Singh expressed confidence that the relationship would grow stronger.

The 'Next Steps in Strategic Partnership' (NSSP) facilitated bilateral trade in high technology[18]. On 12 January 2004 Bush announced expanded engagement on nuclear regulatory and safety issues, missile defence, ways to enhance cooperation in peaceful uses of space technology, and steps to create the appropriate environment for successful high technology commerce. To combat the proliferation of weapons of mass destruction, relevant laws, regulations and procedures would be strengthened, and measures to increase bilateral and international cooperation in this area employed. These cooperative efforts would be undertaken in accordance with the national laws and international obligations of both countries.

New Delhi persuaded Washington to lift restrictions on American exports to India of dual – use high technology goods, to increase civilian space and nuclear cooperation and missile defence. India regarded progress on these issues necessary for an improved strategic relationship. Regarding the NSSP as a milestone, the Bush administration pointed out that 90 per cent of dual-use licensing applications by India were approved in 2003. Then in June 2003, the US-India High-Technology Group was inaugurated. Increased high-technology commerce, export controls, tariff and non-tariff barriers were discussed. Despite some concern in Congress that civilian nuclear and space cooperation would result in the development by India of military nuclear and space programmes, the Bush government believes that such cooperation will be well within the limits outlined by multilateral non-proliferation regimes.

On 17 September 2004 the implementation began of the first phase of the NSSP plan to address proliferation controls and ensure compliance with US export controls. Nuclear non-proliferation remains a sticking point. The nuclear issue has transformed the relationship. Indians thought their standing had risen in the US, but were irritated that the US would not choose India over Pakistan or cooperate with New Delhi at the same level that it did with Beijing. New Delhi was resentful that the US gave authoritarian China access to high technology, but not to India, and that it would discuss nuclear reactors to produce electricity with China – something it would not discuss with India.

High-level meetings were held in August 2003 on joint security issues and missile defence workshops as a follow-on to the June 2003 Multinational Ballistic Missile Defence Conference in Kyoto. There were joint military exercises to combat terrorism. Military Cooperation Groups have been set up to coordinate military exercises; Security Cooperation Groups to coordinate sales and licensing; Joint Technical Groups to coordinate research and development. The Bush administration sees India as a strategic opportunity for the US[19]. There has been cooperation between the FBI, US Customs and Indian Intelligence and Customs to control diversion of opium from legal to illicit uses and to check smuggling. In October 2001 both countries signed a Mutual Legal Assistance Treaty to counter criminal activities, and in April 2002 a cyber security forum was held to increase bilateral cooperation. India and the US have also cooperated on law enforcement, which has increased the sharing of information.

In the wake of India's nuclear explosion in 1998 many Indian goods were scrutinised under American licensing requirements. They included the Indian Space Research Organisation, the Department of Atomic Energy, the Defence Research and Development Organisation, and missile production. In September 2004, as part of the implementation of the NSSP, the US removed the Indian Space Research Organisation from the Entity list, following which India anticipates a three-fold increase in the value of American high-technology imports. Earlier, in June 2004 a conference on space, science and commerce was held in Bangalore, where the Bush government made known its approval of a license authorising the development, jointly with the Indian Space Research Organisation, of Boeing Satellite Systems.

Differences on international issues, including America's refusal to label Pakistan as a terrorist state, and India's refusal to sign the nuclear non-proliferation treaty did not altered the friendly exchanges. In July 2003, India refused an American request for 17,000 troops to be used in Iraq, since the American intervention had not been legitimised by the UN Security Council. An Indian contingent would have been the second largest after that of the US. The Americans were disappointed; they had hoped India would take a different decision, but the Bush administration treated 'this particular outcome' of India's democratic processes 'with respect'[20], in contrast to the angry exchanges that invariably followed any Indian refusal to do Washington's bidding during the Cold War. US officials say that 9/11 turned India and the US into neighbours, with American troops engaged in Afghanistan against the Al Qaeda. Washington sees both countries seeking a regional environment free of terrorism and subversion. There is agreement on stabilising Afghanistan and Iraq. Washington and New Delhi would like democracy to take off in both countries. India has offered help in the reconstruction of Iraq and Afghanistan.

Are India, the US and Pakistan on the Same Side in the War Against Terrorism?

It could be asked whether the Bush administration is looking at the Indo-US relationship after 9/11 through rose-tinted spectacles. A case could be made that Pakistan's role as a frontline state in the anti-Taliban war prevented a major breakthrough in Indo-US ties. New Delhi was quick to point out that since the 1950s, Pakistan had always used American arms against India. In December 2004, New Delhi warned that the sale of F-16s to Pakistan would impair Indo-US relations. The US did not grant Pakistan's request for F-16s, and Secretary for Defence Donald Rumsfeld spoke of expanding military cooperation with India.

American pressure on Pakistan to stop cross-border infiltration into India has not yielded results. Nor has Pakistan made any commitment to stop the training of terrorists. The Bush administration has also been unable to persuade Musharraf to separate political differences over Kashmir from his condonation of terrorism. Visiting Washington and London in December 2004, Musharraf underlined that solutions to Kashmir – and Palestine – were linked to the reducing of terrorism. His attitude implied that Pakistan would continue to justify its training of terrorists and infiltration into Jammu & Kashmir. This will remain an irritant in Indo-US relations as New Delhi takes the view that American aid to Pakistan only encourages Pakistan's belligerence on Kashmir, which in turn is its pretext to train terrorists.

India would like to see $150 billion worth of American investment in its economy. Kashmir – and Pakistan – remain sticking points, and India has been quick to point out that new arms supplies to Pakistan will only be used against India.

That, say the Indians, has been borne out by history. Before 2001, the US transferred two large tranches of arms to Pakistan between 1954-65, and 1981-89[21]. Between the mid-1950s and mid-1960s the US made its largest arms transfer. The *matériel* included F-86 fighters, Patton tanks, artillery, and a submarine on lease, which was the most advanced in South Asia at that time. The possession of such weaponry emboldened Pakistan to try to annex Kashmir in August 1965, and later to cut off the road connecting Jammu to Srinagar.

Between 1981 and 1989 the US gave F-16 aircraft, which were among the most advanced fighters in its armoury. Pakistan also got TOW2 missiles, attack helicopters, and Harpoon missiles for its navy. These arms spurred a race for the most advanced weapons in the subcontinent; they also encouraged Pakistan to complete its nuclear programme. The latest instalment of F-16s, announced in 2005, also displeased India, though it has been agreed that India's reaction has been relatively muted on this occasion[22].

These are some of the reasons why India has made known to the US that another round of F-16 aeroplanes, naval surveillance aircraft and missiles will work against any effort to enhance peace in South Asia. Pranab Mukerjee, currently Indian Defence Minister, has pointed out that these weapons 'are for big wars and not to fight terrorism. Nobody uses F-16s to fight terrorism'[23]. India is also unhappy that these arms have been promised to Pakistan soon after Manmohan Singh announced his government's decision to withdraw some Indian troops from Kashmir.

However, New Delhi may not be averse to American influence over Pakistan. The recent American Intelligence Reform Act, passed by Congress on 9 December 2004, reveals that the US is ready to provide security for Pakistan, help it to sort out its disputes with India, modernise its economy, develop democratic institutions and improve its educational system. Does this represent an attempt to transform Muslim-majority countries like Pakistan – and Afghanistan – in ways that will suit American interests? It does suggest an enduring American military engagement in South Asia, and perhaps also in Iraq and the Middle East. The Act is regarded in New Delhi as the most comprehensive piece of legislation to strengthen American capabilities against Islamic varieties of terrorism[24].

This could be to India's advantage. Because it wants to contain terrorism the US will probably be a moderating influence on Pakistan. However, while that may be acceptable to Musharraf it is hard to gauge the impact of an extended American involvement in Pakistan's domestic domain on his compatriots, not least the clergy and some of his colleagues in the military and intelligence services.

However, Indian scepticism about Pakistan's commitment to ending terrorism is well-founded. Strobe Talbott admitted that the Bush administration had not been 'quite so successful' at persuading Pakistan 'to lay off sponsorship of terrorism … in Kashmir and across the LOC'. He was critical of the gratuitous decision of the Bush administration to grant Pakistan the status of a major non-NATO ally: 'I can't imagine that General Musharraf had ever heard of those initials…And the fact that it was done raised all the bugaboos in India about the US tilt' towards Pakistan since the 1950s, and 'triggered all kinds of unhelpful historical memories'. On top of that, talk about presenting F-16 aircraft to Pakistan 'was more than was necessary', causing 'a lot of repair work' to be done with India[25].

That repair work was accomplished by the Indo-US agreements in March 2006. The anti-Taliban war made the US the dominant foreign influence in South Asia. In one stroke the US asserted that it would remain a major South Asian power and that it had ended its 52 year-old policy of trying to maintain a strategic balance between India and its archenemy Pakistan. That policy only annoyed India while allowing Pakistan to use American arms to destabilize neighbouring countries. Bush ruled out a similar nuclear pact with Pakistan, an American ally since 1954 and a frontline state in the anti-terrorist war, because its history as an unstable '0Islamic' dictatorship differed from that of India[26].

As the only stable South Asian country, India is attractive to the US. Afghanistan is yet to become strong and secure; Pakistan remains unpredictable and a training ground for religious extremists who seek to destabilize Afghanistan and India. In Sri Lanka the prospects of peace between the Sinhalese majority and Tamil minority remain bleak. A Maoist insurgency and royal authoritarianism have made Nepal a collapsed state.

Irritants in the Indo-US relationship will remain, not least because the US refuses to label Pakistan a terrorist state. but the agreements of March 2006 have made it clear that the war on terrorism has put Indo-US relations on a new military and economic footing as the US seeks to enlist India as a strategic associate in crafting a new international arrangement in the twenty-first century.

References

1. Joint Statement of US and India on Terrorism and Bilateral Ties, State Department Washington File, 9 November 2001.

2. http://www.whitehouse.gov/news/releases/2006/03/20060302-9.html; http://www.whitehouse.gov/news/releases/2006/03/20060303-3.html;

3. http://www.whitehouse.gov/news/releases/2006/03/2006302-5html; 'United States, India Continue Cooperation Against Terrorism', State Department Washington File, 25 April 2006.

4. 'Meeting Emerging Security Challenges', transcript of talk by Indian Foreign Secretary Kanwal Sibal at the Carnegie Endowment for International Peace, Washington DC, 4 February 2003.

5. Ambassador Henry Grady in conversation with the State Department, 26 December 1947, cited in my *The Limits of British Influence: South Asia and the Anglo-American Relationship 1947-1956*, p. 58

6. 'P' [Raghavan Pillai], 'Middle Ground between America and Russia: An Indian View', *Foreign Affairs,* Vol. 32, 1954, pp. 261-3.

7. See *Limits of British Influence,* p.29.

8. See my 'India's Relations with Russia and Central Asia', *International Affairs,* Vol. 71, 1995, pp. 69-81.

9. Tarun Khanna and Yasheng Huang , 'Can India Overtake China?' *Foreign Policy.* August/September 2003.

10. http://www.hindustantimes.com/news/5922_1582430,0087.htm.

11. Address by Ambassador Robert Blackwill, 17 July 2003, State Department Washington File: South Asia, 12 August 2003.

12. Indian Defence Minister Jaswant Singh on Jim Lehrer show, 1 October 2001.
    http://64233.167.104/search?q=cache:1qQ_wGuVZecj:
    www.indianembassy.org/special/2001/JS_Online%2520
    NewsHour%2530India@27s%2520Views--
    %2520October%25201,%25201,%25202001.htm+jaswant+singh
    +jim+lehrer+2001&hl=en&i-e=UTF-8

13. *The Hindu,* 18 November 2003.

14. State Department Washington File: South Asia, 12 August 2003. *People, Progress, Partnership,* p. 38.

15. This account is based largely on State Department Washington File: South Asia, 12 July 2003, 12 August 2003, and 13 September 2003.

16. State Department Washington File, 17 March 2004.

17. Brahma Chellaney, 'Systems Upgrade', *Hindustan Times,* 24 September 2004.

18. State Department Washington File, 13 January 2004.

19. State Department Washington File, 12 July 2003.

20. John Lancaster, 'India Refuses US Request for Troops', *The Washington Post,* 14 July 2003.

21. K. Alan Kronstadt, 'Pakistan-US Relations', 11 December 2002, Issue Brief for Congress, especially pp. 5-6.

22. By Ashley Tellis, 'South Asian Seesaw: A New US Policy on the Subcontinent', Policy Brief #38, Carnegie Endowment for International Peace, Washington DC, 2005.

23. This section is based largely on Manoj Joshi, 'Pakistan Gets Nanny: Virtually Becomes US Protectorate,' *Hindustan Times,* 13 December 2004.

24. 'Weapons to Pak Will Hit Peace Bid', ibid.

25. Transcript of talk by Strobe Talbott at the Council of Foreign Relations, New York, on 10 November 2004, http://www.cfr.org/publication_print.php?id=7535&content= See also his book, *Engaging India: Diplomacy, Democracy and the Bomb'* (Washington DC: Brookings Institution Press 2004).

26. http://www.whitehouse.gov/news/releases/2006/03/20060304-2.html.

Chapter 4

Strengthening the Anti-Terrorist Coalition: Can the Kashmir Dispute be Settled?

Kashmir is an area disputed by two nuclear states and affected by international terrorist networks. Not surprisingly, it has earned South Asia the dubious honour of being the most dangerous place on earth. The prevention of war between Pakistan and India over Kashmir may be the most daunting challenge for the US in South Asia, because any conventional war could escalate into a nuclear war.

The American stance on the Kashmir dispute between India and Pakistan is an irritant in Washington's relations with both countries. Kashmir has sparked three wars between India and Pakistan; it is the reason why both exploded the bomb in 1998, why Pakistan has trained terrorists to destabilise Jammu & Kashmir and made it an arena of worldwide *jihad*.[1] Since 9/11, Washington has been aware of Pakistan's connivance in some terrorist attacks on Jammu & Kashmir, New Delhi and Mumbai, but its military compact with Pakistan has prevented it from acquiescing in an Indian request to label Pakistan as a state promoting terrorism.

Never a high priority for the US, South Asia was moved up on Washington's international agenda after India and Pakistan tested atomic bombs in 1998. In 1999, India and Pakistan exchanged artillery fire for ten weeks after extremists supported by Pakistan entered Jammu & Kashmir near the town of Kargil. Fighting broke out between the two countries. American diplomacy helped to end the fighting, and Washington saw itself as the facilitator of dialogue between New Delhi and Islamabad. Again, following terrorist attacks on Indian targets by terrorist organisations based in Pakistan, the US pulled them back from the brink of war early in 2002[2].

Washington is not concerned with the domestic causes or handling of the conflict: only with America's impact on its relations with India and Pakistan and on American interests in the subcontinent. Washington would like to see tensions ease between two friendly countries. The US regards Kashmir as disputed territory – which only annoys India. But its stress on bilateral negotiations to resolve the conflict irks Pakistan, which would prefer international mediation. As the US has been a major player in South Asia since 2001 and is the main moderating foreign influence on Musharraf, it may yet emerge as a catalyst for change on Pakistan's policy on Kashmir.

 The Bush administration shares with India the desire that Kashmir should not become a haven for Islamic militants, but claims that Pakistan does its best to prevent extremist groups based on its soil from crossing the Line of Control that divides the Indian and Pakistani parts of Kashmir. Pakistan, says the State Department, has taken steps to curb infiltration, and Washington has urged Islamabad to redouble its efforts. At the same time, Washington has used its good offices to continue to press India and Pakistan to take confidence-building steps and maintain a dialogue on Kashmir.

Causes of the Kashmir Conflict

The dispute over Kashmir is rooted in the ideological

differences that led to the 1947 partition of British India[3]. The Congress stood for a secular democratic India; the Muslim League, led by Muhammad Ali Jinnah, for a Muslim homeland in the subcontinent, literally a nation-state aligning religion and territory. Given the ethnically diverse populations of the Muslim majority provinces of British India it was impossible to achieve nation-states without war. Civil war triggered the largest flow of refugees seen anywhere since the end of the Second World War, even as the League contented itself with divided Punjab and Bengal – in the famous words of Muhammad Ali Jinnah, with 'a maimed, moth-eaten Pakistan'[4].

Most Hindus and Sikhs left Pakistan in 1947. Today 97 per cent of Pakistan's population is Muslim. The religious definition of Pakistan motivated Pakistan's claim to the princely state of Kashmir in 1947. Kashmir symbolises the ideological schism underlying the 1947 partition of India and Indo-Pakistani animosity to this day: the quarrel over territory reflects their different worldviews and concepts of their respective states. Possession of Kashmir is an integral component of the national identity of both countries. Before the independence and partition of British India in 1947, Kashmir was a princely state. Ninety per cent of its population was Muslim. Hari Singh, the Hindu maharaja of the state in 1947, decided that it should join India, and it acceded to India through an Instrument of Accession in October 1947. The Accession was supported by the National Conference, which was then the largest political party in Kashmir. As protagonists of the religious nation-state, seeking to align the nation with Islam, Pakistan's rulers would not accept this – and never have. To do so would imply that Pakistan was premised on the wrong grounds. If a state with a Muslim majority population could survive in secular India what would be the *raison d'etre* for Pakistan?

Indians, on the other hand, see no reason why a Muslim majority province cannot be included in their secular democratic country: excluding it on religious grounds would negate the ideal of secularism. They also regard the decision taken by Hari Singh placing legality on their side.

Unable to accept the secular logic of Hari Singh's decision, tribesmen from the North-West Frontier Province, trained and supported by the Pakistani army, invaded Kashmir in October 1947. Pakistan sent in its army in May 1948 and hived off one-third of Kashmir and incorporated Gilgit and Baltistan as the 'Northern Territories'. What Pakistan has called 'Azad'(Free) Kashmir comprises only the town of Muzaffarabad and its environs. Most of the territory – about 75 per cent – that Pakistan occupied in 1948 was incorporated as the Northern Terrirtories. It was divided into six districts and its population was diverse. Pakistan has settled Sunnis in the Northern Territories to reduce the proportion of Shias from 95 per cent in 1947 to 50 per cent now. Shia protests against textbooks promoting Sunni versions of Islam sparked sectarian riots in June 2004[5]. The animosity did not end there because Pakistan wanted to annex the whole province as it existed before the partition of India. Pakistan complicated the territorial factor by presenting a slice of Kashmiri territory – Aksai Chin – to China in 1965. This embittered relations between Beijing and New Delhi while doing nothing to improve those between Islamabad and New Delhi.

India and Pakistan have fought three wars over Kashmir – in 1948, 1965 and 1971 – and seemed close to fighting a fourth in 1999. Nuclear tests by both sides in 1998 only reflected their continuing hostility over Kashmir.

Pakistan's claim to Kashmir is part of the reason for its high defence expenditure and also a pretext for its army to dominate its politics. And the absence of religious or political consensus in Pakistan has prevented Islamabad from giving up its claim to Jammu & Kashmir. Rather, Pakistan's rulers, especially the military, have reiterated this claim because it is the one issue on which they can unite Pakistanis and rally them to support the state. The succession of military coups in Pakistan since 1958 is after all, a reminder of the lack of legitimacy of Pakistan's military, its political supremacy, and the absence of consensus in Pakistan.

Kashmir is the reason why India and Pakistan have built arsenals, which include nuclear weapons and ballistic missiles. India blames Pakistan for training cross-border terrorism and secessionist rebels in Jammu & Kashmir. Those, together with strong-arm methods used by Indian forces to quell the trouble in Kashmir, may have claimed anything between 30,000 and 90,000 lives since the insurgency of 1989. Pakistan justifies support to what it calls 'freedom fighters'. High-level meetings between Indian and Pakistani officials in 2001, 2002, 2003 and 2004 have shown no signs of producing a settlement on Kashmir; periods of less tension have alternated with bursts of heightened tension which, in 2002, pushed the two countries to the brink of war. In May 2005, the avoidance of war, rather than peace, appeared to be the best that could be hoped for, especially as Pakistan continued to foster terrorism in Kashmir.

The US would like to see an end to this acrimonious dispute between two countries which it regards as its friends. The domestic handling of both parts of Kashmir is linked to a bilateral settlement, or at least a reduction in tension, between India and Pakistan. So what can the US do to facilitate an end to the conflict?

What are the Alternatives?

The independence of Kashmir has never been on the international agenda: Pakistan is as implacably opposed to independence as India. The constitution of Azad Kashmir (Muzaffarabad) bars from elected office any one who 'propagates against, or takes part in activities prejudicial or detrimental to the ideology of the state's accession to Pakistan'.[5] Election candidates must give written acceptance of Kashmir's accession to Pakistan.

Pro-independence parties such as the United Front of Kashmir (Jammu and Kashmir Muttahida Mahaz), the Jammu & Kashmir Liberation Front (Amanullah Khan), and the Jammu and Kashmir National Awami Front are disqualified from participating in Azad Kashmir's parliamentary elections since they refuse to swear allegiance to Pakistan. Islamabad is repeatedly accused of rigging elections to marginalise pro-independence candidates. Again, Pakistani talk of self-determination implies that a plebiscite should only be held in Jammu & Kashmir. Islamabad seems to assume that Kashmiris in Jammu & Kashmir will choose Pakistan over independence.

Pakistani calls for a plebiscite in Jammu & Kashmir have been spurned, partly because talk of self-determination by a country that has been a dictatorship for most of its history only arouses indignation in India, which has been a democracy since independence. Talk about self-determination infuses moral principles into political quarrels. 'Self-determination' is a contested and ambiguous term[6] and raises for Pakistan the uncomfortable question whether it would agree to the popular vote in all the territories it annexed in 1948, and withdraw its troops from all of them. Given the infructuous dialogue between the two countries over more than fifty years placing this topic on the bilateral agenda may be postponed to the kalends. Since 1947 merely agreeing to talk has constituted a diplomatic achievement; cross-border contacts between the two countries are at the mercy of political red tape, created by ideological and political division.

Also, the UN resolution of 13 August 1948 stated that a plebiscite would be held *after* Pakistan had withdrawn all its troops from Kashmir[7]. Since Pakistan has never done this, India sees no reason why it should agree to a plebiscite. India affirms that the holding of local elections in Jammu & Kashmir, and also the Simla Agreement of 1972, which called for bilateral talks, have superseded the UN resolution. In an attempt to resuscitate democratic processes state elections were held in October 2002, and municipal elections took place in February 2005.

Pakistan has pressed India to hold a plebiscite in Kashmir to ascertain the wishes of the people. The problem is that Pakistan interprets self-determination to mean that Kashmiris will vote to become Pakistanis.

One possibility would be for both sides to accept the Line of Control as an international border. This would be in accordance with the 1972 Simla Agreement. It would also facilitate cross-border contacts across both parts of Kashmir and, more generally, between India and Pakistan. In November 2004, Musharraf reiterated Pakistan's opposition to the idea. Pakistan is a revisionist power and has never given up its claim to the whole province. This is unacceptable to India.

There are also differences in tactics. Pakistan has always welcomed British and American diplomatic intervention over Kashmir since it thinks that their mediation might tilt the scales in its favour. Invoking the principle of sovereignty India has tended to refuse foreign mediation on the grounds that Kashmir is its domestic business. New Delhi regards the West, especially Britain, as part of the problem, since the British, as holders of power in 1947, were responsible for the messy partition that created the Kashmir conflict. There was some justification for this view, as Philip Noel-Baker, then Secretary of State for Commonwealth Relations, committed the British very heavily to Pakistan's position. This annoyed Prime Minister Clement Attlee, who thought Noel-Baker had left the British with no room for manoeuvre. India was angered at Britain's refusal to condemn aggression and contemplated quitting the Commonwealth. Later, in 1953, the American decision to give military aid to Pakistan aroused Indian suspicions of American policy on Kashmir[8]. So India would not trust either Britain and the US to be impartial or just as mediators.

However, India is not necessarily opposed to international facilitation of dialogue with Pakistan. In 1960 the World Bank sponsored the Indus Water Treaty and is the treaty's guarantor. Five years later, the Soviet Union persuaded New Delhi and Islamabad to end the 1965 Indo-Pakistani war with the Tashkent Agreement in January 1966. More recently, in 1999, India did not object to American pressure on Islamabad to disengage from Kargil and to withdraw support for cross-border incursions. American diplomacy helped bring Musharraf and Vajpayee to resume dialogue[9].

Pakistan has tended to welcome international mediation on Kashmir because it anticipates any international influence tilting the scales in its favour. So, in 1999, it was disappointed when, for the first time since 1947, the US described it as the aggressor in Kargil. In 1999 infiltrators, described by Pakistan as 'freedom fighters', crossed the Line of Control from Azad Kashmir and attacked Indian positions near the strategically important Kargil area. India carried out air strikes across the Line of Control to cut off the supply lines of the infiltrators and ejected them. Meeting the then Pakistani Prime Minister, Nawaz Sharif, President Clinton reportedly presented him with evidence that the Pakistani army had deployed nuclear missiles along the Line of Control and pressed him to withdraw the infiltrators. This displeased the army, then headed by Musharraf, who ousted Sharif in a coup in October.

Washington had clearly sided with India and persuaded Islamabad and New Delhi to engage in dialogue. After 9/11, Musharraf allied with the US and provided logistical support for attacks on Taliban Afghanistan, allowed American troops to be stationed on Pakistan's soil and agreed on joint military operations against extremists in its north-western areas bordering Afghanistan. Contrary to Islamabad's expectations, this help did not earn Pakistan American support against India on Kashmir. Musharraf stated in January 2002 that Pakistan would not allow *jihad* in the name of Kashmir. Soon after, however, militant leaders were released and banned extremist organisations allowed to function under new names. Many of them were allowed to move from the Afghan-Pakistani border into Azad Kashmir. The Bush administration conceded New Delhi's allegations about terrorist infiltration from Pakistan into Kashmir.

Musharraf's dilemma was that he had alienated Islamic groups by helping the US against the Taliban, and handing over Taliban and Al Qaeda members to the US. But Washington was displeased at his reluctance to pull down the terrorist network within Pakistan because it was the army's weapon to 'liberate' Kashmir. For their part, Kashmiri extremists noted that he had bowed to American pressure against the Taliban without being able to 'free' Jammu & Kashmir from India. Musharraf ended up annoying the Americans because he was not conforming to their policy of 'zero tolerance' of international terrorism, as well as Kashmiri groups.

Meanwhile, armed militancy in the Kashmir Valley has increased since the late 1980s. The exact number of militants is unknown – they are probably in thousands – and lack a mass base. They are also widely dispersed.

New Delhi has accused Pakistan of giving sanctuary, training and weapons to the terrorist groups who have attacked Indian civilians and security forces in Jammu & Kashmir and Indian cities including New Delhi and Mumbai[10].

The terms and political aims of the terrorist organisations have also changed over time. In the 1980s the Jammu and Kashmir Liberation Front (JKLF), with Kashmiri independence on its agenda, was the leading military group. Terrorist attacks in December 2001 on the Indian parliament, in Kashmir in May 2002 sparked the recall of Indian diplomats from Islamabad and the worsening of tensions along the Indo-Pakistani border. Terrorists killed more than 800 people before the 2002 Kashmiri elections, making it clear that incursions across the Line of Control had never ceased.

American and EU officials are aware anti-Indian terrorist groups are trained and equipped by Pakistan, and have links with Al Qaeda[11]. There may be more than two dozen Islamic militant groups operating inside Jammu & Kashmir; most of them are part of the United Jihad Council, which is based in Azad Kashmir. Since 9/11, the US has listed three organisations, trained in Pakistan and operating in Jammu & Kashmir as terrorists. They included the Harakat-ul-Mujahideen, Al Badr, Haarakat-ul-Jihad-e-Islami and the Jamiat-ul-Mujahideen. The Indian Ministry of Home Affairs has branded them all as terrorist organisations[12]. Comprising Afghan and Al Qaeda veterans, they disapproved of Pakistan's alignment with the US against the Taliban. Kashmiri militants have always been suspicious of Pakistan's motives on Kashmir. Jaish-e-Muhammad claimed responsbility for the suicide bomb attack, in October 2001, on the Jammu & Kashmir State Assembly building in Srinagar. The two groups behind the 13 December attack were the Jaish-e-Muhammad and Lashkar-e-Taiba. Both are supported by several religious seminaries in Pakistan. The Lashkar-e-Taiba seeks to restore Islamic rule all over the subcontinent and sent suicide missions to blow up military cantonments in parts of Jammu & Kashmir. It is based in Muzaffarabad (Azad Kashmir) and near Lahore, and is anti-American and anti-Indian[13]. Another group, the Hizbul Mujahideen, includes many Kashmiris and has been willing to enter into talks with India. It is the militant branch of the Jamiat-e-Islami which is Pakistan's largest political party and a prominent member of the MMA.

The Harakat and the Jaish-e-Mohammad, based in Peshawar and Muzzafarbad, are partners of the Jamiat-e-Ulema-e-Islami Fazlur Rehman group, which is part of the MMA coalition in Pakistan's National Assembly.

Indian Kashmiri groups in Jammu & Kashmir have been willing to do a deal with India; others want independence for Kashmir, not incorporation into Pakistan. The possibility of peace between New Delhi and Kashmiri militants makes Islamabad twitchy – and prompts it - or sections of its intelligence and army – to connive in the organisation of new extremist attacks on India.

Pakistani attempts to sever Kashmir have failed partly because India has been able to hold on to the state; partly because the extremist groups trained by Pakistan comprise Afghan rebels for whom *jihad* in Kashmir is part of a global crusade. They do not empathise with Pakistan's interest in 'self-determination'.

The Hurriyat Conference is more moderate, but divided on its objectives, strategy and tactics. The Hurriyat have entered into negotiations with New Delhi. None of the parties has a mass base, so violence is the only way in which they can shore up their political standing. If and when that strategy has failed they have engaged in dialogue. The Hurriyat refused to take part in elections, partly because it lacked the organisation for this.

Musharraf assured the US in 2002, and again in May 2003, that cross-border terrorism would stop, and that training camps in Pakistan would be closed down. But in July 2004, Deputy Secretary of State Richard Armitage confirmed that the infrastructure in Pakistan that supported terrorism and cross-border activities in Kashmir had not been dismantled[14].

The extremist attacks sparked a new diplomatic row. India and Pakistan alerted their million troops along the Line of Control, raising the spectre of war. Worried that a conventional war could escalate into a nuclear war, the Bush administration worked hard to defuse the tension. While India expelled the Acting Pakistani High Commissioner, Jaleel Abbas Jilani, and four of his colleagues on the grounds that they had funded Kashmiri separatists. Islamabad retaliated by expelling Ambassador Sudhir Vyas for engaging in actions 'unbecoming' of his status – implying spying. Eight days later the ambassadors were allowed to return to their posts, but given that Pakistan's claim to Kashmir is linked to its *raison d'étre* official talks alone will not ease the mistrust and intense bitterness. But the dialogue must continue.

Washington's aim, therefore, is to avert further conflict. It has tried to impress upon Islamabad that good relations with the US will hinge, among other things, on a sustained Pakistani effort to end infiltration by terrorists into the Kashmir Valley. The strong showing made by the MMA in Pakistan's 2002 election made it harder for Musharraf to control militant incursions into Jammu & Kashmir. Whether the US can persuade Islamabad to stop backing Kashmir terrorists is not just a military issue but a political one. Only then will any future talks between India and Pakistan stand any chance of making progress.

Washington has pressed Musharraf to cut off aid to terrorist groups operating in Kashmir. But it has rejected India's demand to condemn Pakistan as a state sponsoring terrorism.

Domestic and International Concerns: Pakistan's Handling of Azad Kashmir and the Northern Territories

International conflicts have domestic roots so Pakistan's training of extremists who have made incursions into Jammu & Kashmir is best understood in relation to its handling of the Northern Territories and Azad Kashmir, and also its domestic politics. Pakistan's training of Islamic militants is linked to its religious definition. For Pakistanis, without the inclusion of Jammu & Kashmir their country is incomplete. Moreover, the fragility of its political institutions and, the political dominance of its military also explain its illiberal governance of the Kashmiri territories it annexed in 1948. How Pakistan has governed the areas it occupied is important to an understanding of Indian indignation at calls for a plebiscite in Jammu & Kashmir.

There can be no solution to the Kashmir problem without greater democratisation in Pakistan, Azad Kashmir and the Northern Territories. Azad Kashmir and the Northern Territories cannot be more democratic than the rest of Pakistan. Despite its so-called independence the term Azad Kashmir is a fig leaf for tight control by Islamabad. Any move towards democracy in Pakistan must include not only Azad Kashmir but Gilgit and Baltistan, which were annexed by Pakistan after 1947. The Northern Territories have never been granted self-rule nor are they constitutionally a part of Pakistan. This implies that the people of the Northern Territories are stateless, although the area is administered by a high-level Pakistani official. Half a century under Pakistan's strong-arm methods have bred hostility towards Islamabad. This is why any American talk of 'normalcy' in Kashmir jars on Indian nerves.

The Council for Azad Kashmir is chaired by the Pakistani prime minister. The top officials are deputed by Islamabad, which in effect means that the Pakistani military orders the Azad Kashmir parliament on all policies. This is done through the Ministry of Kashmir Affairs and Northern Areas and States and Frontier Regions (hereafter the Ministry of Kashmir Affairs) and the Azad Jammu and Kashmir Council.[15] The Council's decisions cannot be challenged by the Supreme Court of this 'independent' region or by any court in Pakistan. Under the 1974 constitution, Islamabad can dismiss an elected government in Azad Kashmir. Islamabad's approval of all legislation passed by the Azad Kashmir assembly – including that on the budget and appointments – is necessary and Islamabad pays 90 per cent of Azad Kashmir's budget.

American advice on easing Indo-Pakistani tensions should, therefore, include political liberalisation in Azad Kashmir and the Northern Territories. Democracy is about accommodating differences peacefully. But it is hard to see this happening given the military's right to dismiss any Pakistani government in the first place. Therefore, will the US be able to persuade Pakistan to open debate on amending the 1974 constitution, lift restrictions on the powers of the Azad Jammu and Kashmir Council, and restrict Islamabad's authority over the Azad Kashmir parliament, and the right to dismiss its government?

Unlike Azad Kashmir, which has an interim constitution, the constitutional status of the Northern Areas has never been determined, and its residents are not represented in the national legislature. The Ministry of Kashmir Affairs oversees all policy and administration there. Washington could advise Islamabad to reduce its military presence in the Northern Territories, start talks on the 1999 Supreme Court decision to grant the Northern Territories constitutional status and representation in the national legislature. Politicians from both Azad Kashmir and the Northern Territories could participate in such talks. The rule of law should be strengthened by the creation of a court of appeals, under the Northern Areas Council Legal Framework Order 1994 and the 16 December 2003 order of the Supreme Court. The establishment of a Public Services Commission for the Territories could be the first step towards professionalising governance there.

American advice to Islamabad on stamping out sectarian violence could extend to the Northern Territories. Like the rest of Pakistan, the area has seen sectarian violence between Sunnis and Shias. Once again, the crux of the matter is the absence of consensus in Pakistan.

Within Pakistan

Domestic politics have contributed significantly to shaping Pakistan's Kashmir policy, with successive administrations playing the Kashmir card for political gain. Successive Pakistani governments, especially those headed by military rulers, have lacked legitimacy. Kashmir provides them with a pretext to rally their compatriots. They have often displayed a more uncompromising attitude on Kashmir than their civilian counterparts. The military also use the dispute to justify high defence expenditures, including a costly nuclear programme and interventions in politics. The conflict with India reinforces the army's self-appointed role as the nation's sole guardian against an aggressive and nuclear-armed neighbour.

The military establishment has repeatedly disrupted, or even reversed, attempts by civilian governments to adopt a more moderate approach towards India. Benazir Bhutto's first government tried to improve relations, establishing confidence-building measures with Prime Minister Rajiv Gandhi. These included the agreements on the Prohibition of Attack against Nuclear Installations and Facilities and establishment of a prime ministerial hotline. Bhutto, who threatened the military's hard-line strategy towards its perennial adversary, was eventually dismissed by President Ghulam Ishaq Khan, who was close to General Zia-ul-Haq. Similarly, Nawaz Sharif's overtures to India during his second government, culminating in the Lahore Declaration of February 1999, were blocked by the army's incursions into Kargil. Sharif's decision to withdraw from Kargil estranged the military establishment, leading eventually to the October 1999 coup.

The post-1989 unrest in Jammu & Kashmir, managed heavy-handedly, has added a more radical Islamic dimension to the Kashmir dispute. Kashmiri and non-Kashmiri militants raised the conflict's political, military and economic costs for India, and the insurgency gave India a bad international press. Islamabad makes no secret of its support for local rebels; this support really implies backing for the extremists and their training, which are axioms of its Kashmir policy. At the January 2004 SAARC Summit, held in Islamabad, President Musharraf pledged that Pakistani territory would not be used for terrorist activity[16], tacitly acknowledging Pakistan's support of, and connivance in, terrorist attacks in Jammu & Kashmir. He subsequently insisted on making a distinction between terrorists and freedom fighters[17] and said that Pakistan would 'continue' to support Kashmiri self-determination. He stressed that the Kashmir liberation struggle was not terrorism and Kashmiris were fighting for a just cause.

Quite unsurprisingly, it did not take long for India to complain, yet again, and to present evidence of, training camps in Azad Kashmir and a rise in the number of terrorist activities, organised across the border[18]. But in September

2004, Prime Minister Manmohan Singh observed that the infrastructure of terrorism remained intact, and that its dismantling could pave the way for bilateral discussions on several issues.

The US could urge Musharraf to demonstrate to India and the international community a genuine determination to curb extremism in Kashmir by stopping all support to militants in Jammu & Kashmir, launching a more intensive effort to crack down on extremist organisations in Pakistan, preventing use of its territory for training extremists, and stopping infiltration across the Line of Control.

Kashmir remains a critical issue between India and Pakistan. Both will need to make several major changes to their policies if they wish to lay the groundwork for peace. Pakistan must give up its support for militancy, work intensively to disband militant groups and recognise that its policy has not only led to intense suffering for the Kashmiri people but has undermined stability at home.

India has blamed the problems in Jammu & Kashmir on externally-driven terrorism but it is also aware that its handling of the state has at times been maladroit. The holding of elections in October 2002 was intended as a first step to restoring normal administrative processes. It was an attempt to undo the harm done by the rigging of elections by Rajiv Gandhi's government in 1987 with a view to defeating the National Conference, a moderate political party. This ploy appears mystifying. In regional and all-India elections held in 1967 and 1972 the Congress polled 53 and 55.4 per cent of the vote respectively, while the National Conference obtained 46.2 and 47.3 per cent, respectively, in the elections of 1977 and 1983. In a state in which 90 per cent of the population is Muslim, the performance of Muslim communal parties – the Muslim United Front and the Jamiat-e-Islami – was dismal. Together they obtained 7.2 per cent of the votes in 1972, 3.6 per cent in 1977, and 20 per cent in 1987. Essentially, the elections showed a fairly well functioning democracy in Kashmir, and it was the deliberate distortion of democratic norms by Rajiv Gandhi's government that caused disillusionment with Indian democracy and provoked separatism[19]. Intervention by Pakistan, a fuller discussion of which is beyond the scope of this book, also contributed to the uprising of 1989, and India still faces an uphill task in restoring normalcy to the state. Several attempts to hold elections before October 2002 failed in the face of separatist threats.

The relatively free and fair elections to the state assembly in September and October 2002, and the defeat of the ruling National Conference showed that New Delhi was doing its best to normalise the situation in Kashmir. The US welcomed the elections and was encouraged by its results. The defeat of the National Conference meant that for the first time since 1947 it would be out of power. The elections were won by a coalition comprising the Democratic and Congress parties, led by Mufti Muhammad Sayeed who took over as the new Chief Minister. The success of the People's Democratic Party-Congress coalition of Mufti Muhammad Sayeed has made it easier for the Manmohan Singh government to engage in dialogue with different political groups. As part of the new government in Jammu & Kashmir, the Congress has much at stake in Mufti Muhammad Sayeed's success.

Mufti Muhammad Sayeed said the state needed 'a healing touch' and 'our own version of a Marshall Plan'[20].

He pledged an era of more open government in the state to restore confidence in democratic institutions. He highlighted severe problems of low literacy, weak prospects for employment generation, a lack of foreign investment and power shortages. He also complained that basic services were often unavailable even though Kashmir exceeds the average of Indian states in per capita tax collection. His government adopted a programme aimed at promoting human rights, reconciliation and development. Diplomacy would be the key to implementing them.

In January 2004, talks were held with Kashmiri separatists for the very first time at the highest levels of the Indian government. There was mutual understanding between Vajpayee and Deputy Prime Minister L.K. Advani about the need to end violence in Kashmir. Since June 2004, Manmohan Singh's government has tried to break the deadlock by repealing the controversial Prevention of Terrorism Act (POTA). This was in accordance with the Common Minimum Programme outlined by the Congress and its electoral allies before the national elections of May 2004. The government wishes to respect the letter and spirit of Article 370 of the Indian Constitution which accords a special status to Kashmir, and to engage in dialogue with all groups in the state. Such steps would enhance Kashmiri confidence in New Delhi's intentions. But whether militants would respect the spirit of dialogue remains to be seen. On 11 November, in a future show of goodwill to both Kashmiris and Pakistan, Manmohan Singh announced that India would reduce the number of troops in Jammu & Kashmir.

What was achieved by the Delhi talks in September 2004? If India wants to suggest something new it should be the holding of free and fair elections in the Northern

Territories. Asking New Delhi to conduct a plebiscite falls flat on Indian ears since Pakistan has been a dictatorship for most of its history and has incorporated most of the Kashmiri territory captured in 1948 without introducing democracy. The democratisation of Azad Kashmir and the Northern Territorism should be discussed by India and Pakistan at political summits.

Kashmir has always troubled the US. Washington seems to think that Pakistan, in particular, would be a better ally if it could free its military resources from their onerous tasks in Kashmir. Pakistan's unreliability as an ally stems from its domestic instability which results from years of military rule which both reflects, and has created, an absence of consensus on the nature of the Pakistani state. Pakistan's military has to free itself from domestic politics if it is to contribute more substantially to America's international policing.

Why has it been so difficult for the US to facilitate dialogue and what can it do to normalise relations? India will not accept American – or foreign – advice on establishing forms of dialogue with local Kashmiri groups because it has continually kept the channels of communication open. New Delhi is aware that normalcy in Kashmir must include better governance to enhance the trust of Kashmiris in the administration. India, as a democracy, realises that peace is necessary for the economic development which would address some of the root causes of militancy.

Peace in Kashmir and reduction of tensions between India and Pakistan require a sustained, long-term effort by many parties and extensive dialogue to rebuild trust and get all parties to tackle the most contentious issues. There is also little likelihood of compromise until much more has been done to improve the lives of Kashmiris that have been so damaged by conflict.

Key CBMs initiated between India and Pakistan since their last full-scale war in 1971[21] included the establishment, in 1965, of a hotline between Military Operations Directorates; an agreement, signed in 1988, on the Prohibition of Attack against Nuclear Installations and Facilities. The Agreement was ratified and implemented in 1992. The year 1989 saw the establishment of a hotline between Prime Ministers Rajiv Gandhi and Benazir Bhutto. In 1991 India and Pakistan signed an agreement on Advance Notice of Military Exercises, Manoeuvres, and Troop Movements; and, in 1992, another agreement on measures to Prevent Air Space Violations and to Permit Overflights and Landing by Military Aircraft.

While these initiatives were sound in themselves, mistrust between Islamabad and New Delhi prevented their successful implementation. For example, both countries accused each other of spreading misinformation through the hotlines. Similarly, neither can verify the accuracy of the information even as they have continued to exchange lists of nuclear facilities under the 1988 agreement. In August 1999, India shot down a Pakistani aircraft it claimed had entered its airspace, an allegation Pakistan denied. There is no mechanism to address differences, let alone to discuss and implement remedies.

Sometimes negotiations fail even before they start. For example, the summit meeting between Prime Ministers Atal Bihari Vajpayee and Nawaz Sharif at Lahore in February 1999 was undermined by the conflict that Pakistan's military, then headed by Musharraf, provoked soon afterwards at

Kargil. Subsequently, as President Musharraf met Vajpayee at Agra in 2001 but the talks broke down. Pakistan's connivance in the militant attack on the Indian parliament in December 2001 exacerbated the tension and pushed the countries to the brink of war, and Washington worked hard to ease the stalemate.

Washington was, therefore, pleased that Vajpayee offered an olive branch to Pakistan on 18 April 2003. Fresh attempts were made to mend fences with Pakistan. High Commissioners (ambassadors) resumed their posts. But in September a fresh outburst of violence sparked heated exchanges between Vajpayee and Musharraf. Vajpayee tried to revive peacemaking by proposing contact between people of the Indian and Pakistani parts of Kashmir. Musharraf's reponse was positive. In November, India and Pakistan agreed to a ceasefire along the Line of Control and on the Siachen glacier. By early January 2004 all air, bus and train links had been restored. Meeting for the first time since July 2001 at the twelfth summit of the South Asian Association for Regional Cooperation (SAARC) in Islamabad in January 2004, Musharraf and Vajpayee started a 'composite dialogue', which would include Kashmir and the peaceful settlement of all bilateral issues.

The surprise defeat of Vajpayee's government in the Indian election in April 2004 raised questions over the future of the peace process. The new Prime Minister, Manmohan Singh, and the then Foreign Minister, Natwar Singh, were cautiously constructive. The Lahore and Agra meetings raised expectations but resulted in disappointment. Manmohan Singh and Musharraf agreed to continue the 'composite dialogue' set in train in January 2004, which would cover all contentious issues including Kashmir. Their

Foreign Secretaries met in New Delhi to discuss issues of peace, security and Kashmir on 27-28 June and again in early September 2004.[6] In July Natwar Singh paid his first visit to Pakistan to attend the ministerial meeting of the SAARC. The new Congress-led government's agreement to continue talks with Pakistan has raised expectations. But the dialogue did not mark a turning point in relations between the long- time adversaries: a settlement on Kashmir remained distant.

Tensions continually have to be defused; the process of dialogue can easily be thrown off the rails. The discussion and establishment of closer ties in less controversial areas such as trade, air links and cooperation in trade could help build domestic constituencies for peace. Such talks are more likely to succeed at the bilateral level, but the US should encourage them while being aware that they may not necessarily be a prologue to more amicable handling of Kashmir.

What concrete measures emerged from the meeting between Musharraf and Manmohan Singh in September 2004? On 21 October Musharraf made three new suggestions to defuse tension over Kashmir[22].

First, Pakistan would give up its demand for a plebiscite, while it was 'allergic' to making the Line of Control a permanent border. Musharraf called for the demilitarisation of, and autonomy for, the whole of Kashmir, which could be put under the joint control of both India and Pakistan. Musharraf's plan identified seven regions of Kashmir and dealt with the state on the basis of its ethnic schisms and not religion. Some parts could be divided between the two countries and the Valley could either become autonomous or put under UN supervision.

All these alternatives would involve the drawing of new boundaries.

Autonomy would have to be guaranteed, and Kashmiri sovereignty accepted, by both countries. Somewhere there would have to be an international border – even if Pakistan does not want the Line of Control as one. Pakistan does not wish to give up its claim to the whole of Kashmir.

Washington responded by reiterating that Kashmir was a bilateral issue and welcomed Musharraf's initiative. But in New Delhi officials doubted the seriousness behind Musharraf's proposals, partly because they were only aired in the media. And his 'plan' found few takers, partly because India will not agree to any redrawing of borders. Does Musharraf's concept of autonomy mean identical autonomy for all of Kashmir, including Jammu & Kashmir, Azad Kashmir and the Northern Territories? How would this be developed in Azad Kashmir and the Northern Territories given that both have different political status and institutions? Identical autonomy would only be possible if free and fair elections took place on both sides of the Line of Control, but such elections are not the norm in Pakistan and have never been held in the Northern Territories. Indian commentators observed that Pakistan had changed the demographic composition of Azad Kashmir and the Northern Territories with Punjabi, Pashtun and Mirpuri settlers[23].

Within Pakistan public reaction to Musharraf's plan was discouraging. That fact alone made New Delhi wary of taking it seriously. His ideas were turned down by the Jamiat-e-Islami, various *jihadi* groups, and most political parties. Musharraf had to reassure his compatriots that the plan is not a sell-out to India, that Pakistan would never compromise the interests of Kashmir, and that the Line of Control would not be accepted as an international border.

Joint control could only be established if Indo-Pakistani relations were amicable. That would have to include agreement that a jointly-controlled Kashmir would not be a conduit for terrorists to move from one country to another. The concerns of each country on terrorism would need discussion. Normalcy must include the prior establishment of trade relations and free movement of peoples. Only then could there be any certainty that Kashmir would not be a haven for terrorists.

By the end of 2004 it was clear that dialogue over confidence-building measures had got nowhere. In October, India presented new points for discussion: Pakistan has yet to respond to them. Pakistani officials visiting Jammu & Kashmir that month claimed that leaders of the Hurriyat Conference opposed the establishment of a bus linking Srinagar and Muzaffarabad since that would encourage a settlement based on the status quo. The Foreign Ministers – Khurshid Kasuri and Natwar Singh – agreed on the easing of visa restrictions, and on the possible sharing by India of a gas pipeline from Iran to Pakistan. In return for participation in the pipeline project, India wanted Pakistan to confer Most Favoured Nation Treatment on its exports. Pakistan refused. India also demanded that its goods destined for Afghanistan be allowed transit through Wagah and Lahore. Until then Indian goods, sent through Karachi, had been mysteriously held up there for eight months, so they were sent through the Iranian port of Bandar Abbas to Herat. Aziz insisted that the pipeline project stood on its own, and was not part of the composite dialogue[24].

India and Pakistan also fell out over the conditions under which the road between Srinagar and Muzaffarabad should be opened. India favoured the use of the road by non-Kashmiris; it also wanted Kashmiris crossing the Line of Control to carry passports for security reasons. Pakistan rejected these demands. On 15 December, Islamabad demanded that both countries aim at parity in military strength. This would involve the dismantling of almost half of the Indian army[25]. The exchanges, then, only seemed to have created a new impasse.

The US could advise Pakistan to give up its claim to the whole province. The claim is dubious, given the history of the province. Religion inspired the creation of Pakistan but it has not forged consensus, and Pakistan's own handling of the Kashmiri territories it annexed in 1948 has not been based on democratic norms. That would require greater political liberalisation in Pakistan.

India will not change its stance on the Line of Control unless Pakistan changes its attitude on resumption of bus services and trade links. Meanwhile, acceptance of the Line of Control would usher in the stability needed to improve the life chances of Kashmiris on both sides of the border. It would also allow both countries to strengthen transport and trade links across the border. And it would pave the way for talks on meeting the UN recommendation that people belonging to kin ethnic groups should be allowed to have contact with each other across international borders[26].

Washington should also press on Pakistan at least to accept the Line of Control as an international border and give up its claim to self-determination – especially one that cannot be realised. Waving the flag of self-determination in the hope that Kashmiris will vote to become Pakistanis only keeps the pot boiling without offering any good to ordinary Kashmiris. A secure border could facilitate travel and the strengthening of ties between Kashmiris on both sides of the Line of Control, and would go a long way in normalising relations between India and Pakistan.

If Islamabad dropped its insistence on annexing the whole of Kashmir both India and Pakistan could reduce their military presence along the Line of Control and stabilise the ceasefire. Contacts across the Line of Control could then be increased.

Conclusion

The anti-terrorist front will not be strengthened by an early resolution of the Kashmir conflict. Were the peace talks between Musharraf and Manmohan Singh early in 2005, Singh's olive branch in March 2006, the inauguration of a bus service from Amritsar to Nankana Sahib, holy cities of the Sikhs in India and Pakistan respectively, in April 2006, confidence-building measures or just another series of pleasantries? Especially in the wake of India's rejection of a Pakistani proposal that it remove heavy weapons from Jammu & Kashmir on the grounds that it has the sovereign right to deploy troops on its territory? A series of terrorist attacks in Kashmir on the eve of the second roundtable conference on Kashmir in May suggested that terrorists with links to Pakistan were trying yet again block any possibility of a negotiated settlement.[27] Both India and Pakistan will continue to try to get the US on their side; both will be irritated by what Washington sees as its evenhandedness. Nevertheless, the US has been able to get military help from Pakistan and will continue to wage war against militants on the Afghan-Pakistani border.

But America's alliance with Pakistan will remain a

double-edged sword. Pakistan cannot give up its religious identity, but can it give up the irredentism and extremism that are among its offshoots? Only then will Musharraf's version of 'moderate' Islam have meaning; only then will it defuse tension over Kashmir. That, in turn will hinge on his ability to steer certain sections of the Pakistani army and intelligence. India regards Pakistan as the 'epicentre' of international terrorism. Britain, the US, France and Russia have all called on Pakistan to stop acting as the springboard for terrorist incursions into Kashmir and to dismantle the infrastructure of terrorism[28]. Kashmir will remain a sticking point between India and Pakistan. The US has different uses for different countries in maintaining the anti-terrorist front. To preserve and strengthen the coalition all that the US can do is to continue to facilitate the dialogue between New Delhi and Islamabad over Kashmir. It could yet emerge as a catalyst for change in Kashmir.

References

1. 'Jammu & Kashmir' refers to the Indian part of Kashmir. For a recent account of Pakistan's attitude to Kashmir see Husain Haqqani, *Pakistan: Between Mosque and Military* (Washington DC, Carnegie Endowment for International Peace, 2005), pp. 261-309.

2. This is an American claim. In June 2002 diplomatic intervention by Defence Secretary Donald Rumsfeld and Deputy Secretary of State Richard Armitage cooled tension between India and Pakistan. Amit Gupta and Kaia Leather, 'Kashmir: Recent Developments and US Concerns', Congressional Service Report, 21 June 2002, p. CRS-1. See also Anwar Iqbal, 'Shuttle Diplomacy Prevented Indo-Pakistan War: Bush', *Dawn,* 23 April 2004, and 'Powell Claims Peace Role in South Asia', *Dawn,* 28 May 2004 respectively.

3. On the partition see Penderel Moon *Divide and Quit',* and my *Origins of the Partition of India, 1936-1947,* both published in *The Partition Omnibus* (Oxford University Press 2002).

4. From the vast literature on Kashmir I would recommend Sumit Ganguly, *The Crisis in Kashmir: Portents of War, Hopes of Peace* (New

York: Cambridge University Press and Washington DC: Woodrow Wilson Centre, 1997); Sumit Ganguly (ed), *The Kashmir Question: Retrospect and Prospect* (London: Frank Cass 2003); Sisir Gupta, *Kashmir: A Study in India-Pakistan Relations* (London and New Delhi: Asia Publishing House 1966). See also my 'Europe's Lesson for South Asia', *Far Eastern Economic Review,* 29 August 2002 and 'Where Does Kashmir End?' *The Times Literary Supplement,* 7 November 1997.

4.   Raj Chengappa, 'In the Forbidden Zone', *India Today,* 30 December 2004.

5.   Azad Jammu and Kashmir Interim Constitution Act 1974, Article 7(2).

6.   For a good overview of this controversial topic see Antonio Cassese, *Self-Determination of Peoples: A Legal Appraisal* (Cambridge: Cambridge University Press 1995).

7.   UNCIP Resolution of August 13, 1948 (S/1100 Para 75). http://www.indiagov.org/policy/Kashmir/uncip%28s1100%29.htm.

8.   See my *Limits of British Influence,* p. 29.

9.   Alan Sipress and Thomas Ricks, 'Report: India, Pakistan Were Near Nuclear War in '99, *The Washington Post,* 15 May 2002, and 'Kashmir: Recent Developments and US Concerns', CRS-5.

10. John Lancaster, 'India Shocked by Bombay Bombings and Suspects', 12 September 2003.

11. See the statements by British Foreign Secretary Jack Straw, 10 June 2002, French Foreign Minister Dominique de Villepin, 29 March 2003 and Nancy Powell, cited in 'Kashmir: The True Story', http://meaindia.nic.in/jk/19jk01.pdf.

12. http://mha.nic.in/poto-02.htm#schedule, cited in CRS report on *Terrorism in South Asia,* 9 August 2004, pp. CRS-18.

13. State Department, *Patterns of Global Terrorism,* 30 April 2003.

14. State Department Washington File, 15 July 2004.

15. See the recent article by Raj Chengappa, 'In the Forbidden Zone', *India Today,* 30 December 2004; and http://www.pakistan.gov.pk/kashmiraffairs-division/about division/overview.

16. http://www.infopak.gov.pk/press_President_06Jan2004_saarc.htm.

17. Musharraf's address to Azad Kashmir Legislative Assembly, 6

February 2004, http://www.infopak.gov.pk/President_Address/Address_Azad_Jammu_Kashmir_Legislative_Assembly.htm

18. *India Today,* 12 September 2004, pp. 38-44.

19. Inder Singh, *Democracy, Ethnic Diversity and Security in Postcommunist Europe,* p. 41.

20. Speech at 50th National Development Council meeting, 21 December 2002, cited in 'India/Pakistan Relations and Kashmir: Steps Towards Peace', International Crisis Group Asia Report no. 79, 24 June 2004.

21. The following account is based largely on Swati Pandey and Teresita Schaffer, 'Building Confidence in India and Pakistan', *South Asia Monitor* No. 49, Centre for Strategic and International Studies, Washington DC, 1 August 2002.

22. BBC Report 26 October 2004.

23. K. Subrahmanyam, 'A Step Forward: Moving on Musharraf's Condominium Proposal', *The Times of India,* 22 November 2004. See also G. Parthasarthy, 'Through a Kashmiri Gate', *Hindustan Times,* 28 October 2004; Vikram Sood, "Khaki Diplomacy", ibid., 8 December 2004, and Michael Binyon, 'Where There's a Will', ibid., 30 October 2004.

24. Prem Shankar Jha, 'Mutual Mistrust Fund', *Hindustan Times,* 30 December 2004.

25. Ibid.

26. *Declaration on the Rights of Persons Belonging to National or Ethnic, Religious and Linguistic Minorities,* United Nations General Assembly Resolution, 47/135, 18 December 1992.

27. See *The Tribune,* 19 March and 2 May 2006; *The Hindu,* 2 May 2006, BBC Report, 27 April 2006, http://news.bbc.co.uk/2/hi/south_asia/4952404stm, and G. Parthasarathy, 'Pugwash Message: Concentrate on Areas of Common Interest', *The Tribune,* 23 March 2006.

28. Statement by CIA Director George Tenet Before Senate Armed Services Committee, 'Worldwide Threat: Converging Dangers in a Post-9/11 World', 19 March 2002.

Conclusion: Looking Forward

In August 2004 George Bush admitted that the 'war on terrorism' could not be won.[1] The Taliban were overthrown, but Osama bin Laden, the prime mover behind 9/11, remains at large, probably in Pakistan. The war on terrorism remains a war without front lines or geographical or legal definition. Even if an international consensus emerges on a definition of terrorism[2], it is a war against an enemy with an elusive identity. And security against terrorism cannot be taken for granted in any part of the world: Al Qaeda attacked ten states on four continents in the last five years. Al Qaeda or its associates have committed acts of terrorism in Indonesia, Turkey, Morocco and Spain. They have been damaged but not eradicated. New terrorist groups have emerged since 2001, old ones resuscitated. Alliances between *jihadist* groups are continually made, unmade and remade. Military means have to be used, if only because it is hard to talk and negotiate with terrorists pointing guns at you.

Most states have been created by war, but the disintegration of the USSR showed that they could not necessarily be sustained by force. In many post-communist countries democracy has been a method of state-building; that method is being tried in Afghanistan after the defeat of the Taliban.

Since the campaign against terrorism is simultaneously one for democratic values, the means used by the US remain important. The end of the Cold War established democracy as the only legitimising ideology of international society, and the fight against terrorism has confirmed that it is a means to achieve security as well as an end in itself. Some fifteen years after the end of the Cold War democracy-building remains a security issue. The necessity of using force to battle with terrorism only strengthens the need for greater international cooperation to promote tolerance, intellectual and political choice that are intrinsic to democracy; and through them, to enhance peace and economic development which will be the best counterpoises to terrorism. The US's respect for democratic and human rights norms will play an important part in convincing Afghans – and others – of its determination to defeat terrorism by advancing democracy. Its disregard of those norms will only make it lose friends and influence, and weaken the fight against terrorism.

Democracy can only be created within the sovereign state. In the new millennium the state is on the front line in the anti-terrorist campaign[3], but South Asia shows that no country can go it alone, whether it is the US in Afghanistan, or Afghanistan itself, under its fledgling government since 2004. Sovereignty is the keystone of international society, but the network of global terrorism can only be pulled down through international cooperation. Both facts have been borne out in South Asia. The US realised, after 9/11, that its military paramountcy was not synonymous with omnipotence. (Its failures in Iraq have only underlined that). The UN legitimised America's defeat of the Taliban; it was the custodian of the peace process initiated at Bonn in November 2001 and its help will be essential for the democratic reconstruction and development of Afghanistan.

South Asia includes two front line states – Afghanistan and Pakistan – in America's anti-terrorist campaign. South Asian – and international – security are endangered by the Kashmir dispute between India and Pakistan, which, along with Palestine, is a long-standing quarrel which can be exploited as an incitement to terrorism.

The war against the Taliban was fought in the name of enduring freedom. The question this raises in Afghanistan, after its first election in 2004, is whether democracy can be built there. It will require a massive infusion of American military and economic aid for many years to build the political and legal institutions, the economic and educational progress that will keep terrorism at bay.

After 1991, Eastern Europe showed two things: that neither authoritarianism nor force could cement states; and that democracy could take off in countries with weak democratic traditions and be an instrument of state-building[4]. The East European achievement may not be replicated everywhere, but Iraq shows that the fall of a dictator does not mean that democracy can be introduced through the barrel of a democratic superpower's gun. Like many post-conflict countries, Afghanistan cannot choose between guns and butter, if only because remnants of the Taliban and Al Qaeda have to be quashed even as Karzai embarks on development through democratisation which, it is hoped, will tackle the deep-rooted causes of terrorism.

Power comprises two elements: force and consent. If force cannot be sustained, unilaterally and indefinitely, then consent has to be tried – that is where democratic state-building comes into the picture. That means a government chosen through free and fair elections, new legislative institutions, justice and security sector reform and the protection of human rights. In Afghanistan democratic governance will have the added task of confronting, and pushing back, the challenge posed by extremist Islam to

129

international security. The remaking of Afghanistan must not foment new insecurity and potential support for terrorism in the future.

It is impossible to predict how long the war on terrorism will continue, and how the causes of terrorism can be reversed. The defeat of the Taliban created a collapsed state, a power vacuum that has so far been filled partly by the US and its European allies, partly by a fragile government in Kabul and partly by warlords trying to extend their sway over their country. The fall of the Taliban served as America's point of entry into South Asia but it cannot provide an exit strategy from the region. Only a deeper American engagement that addresses not just military issues but also the basic social and economic causes of terrorism will limit the damage done by terrorism in the long run. Is the US prepared for such a long drawn out involvement in Afghanistan? In the summer of 2005 the US claimed to be stepping up its efforts to promote democracy as an antidote to terrorism, and the Joint US-Afghan Declaration for Strategic Partnership of 23 May 2005 suggested an extended American engagement in Afghanistan, but it is too early to predict its course and outcome.

Terrorism does not spring up only in poor countries: the instigators of 9/11 were not poor and highly developed countries including Italy, Germany, Spain and Britain have had to contend with terrorism. Religion was not a significant cause of terrorism in the first three countries. Most terrorists today are Muslims – but all Muslims are not militants. South Asia shows that extremism can be found among Muslims, Hindus, Sikhs and Christians. What is hard to explain is why terrorism has arisen in democratic and rich countries. Neither democracy nor development may in themselves be cures for, or prophylactics of, terrorism. But the search for answers is important if the revival of terrorism is to be nipped in the bud in Afghanistan as democratic governance is built there, brick by brick.

What role will Islam play in containing terrorism in South Asia after December 2004? Islam defines both Afghanistan and Pakistan. But the chances are that their respective leaders will use it in different ways.

In Afghanistan the constitutional ban on religious parties suggests that the country's constitution-makers do not want ethnic and religious sentiment to be used for political mobilisation.

In Pakistan, however, there is no sign that the military, which gives the political lead, will stop using religion for political purposes, whether against its home-grown foes or India. There are several reasons for this. First, Musharraf's linking of the settlement of Kashmir – and Palestine – to the removal of the underlying grievances of terrorism amounts to a condonation of extremism. By analogy, would Britain's handling of Northern Ireland justify Catholic terrorism all over the world?

Secondly, education can help to prevent the spread of extremist ideas. However, in Pakistan, it has been used to instil extremist ideas. Attempts to moderate – whatever that means – the syllabi in *madrasas* – have been lukewarm and ineffectual. Moreover, political education, provided by the military and political parties, is laced with extremist versions of Islam, and has shaped the mindset of Pakistanis.

Musharraf is threatened by extremists, partly—and allegedly – for selling the pass to the US against the Taliban.

The question is whether he is willing or able to grasp the extremist nettle. Despite American coaxing and cajoling, Musharraf gives primacy to religion as a political tool. It is in the interest of the US to continue to persuade him to stop exploiting religion for political ends, domestically and against India. Is Washington's perception of him as a moderate leader trying to promote moderate Islam misconceived? Does his condonation of extremist ideology easily become an exoneration of extremism?

Musharraf has marginalised moderate politicians and parties and will not let them challenge the military's ascendancy. Their own fragmentation and dismal economic and political performance have made it hard for them to win mass support. So the army, simultaneously vulnerable and invincible, dominates Pakistan, probably because it appears to many as the best political bet. The result is that extremist ideology has been institutionalised in Pakistan.

There is evidence, from the many American sources cited in this book, that the Bush administration is aware of the training of terrorists in Pakistan, but persists in praising Musharraf as a steadfast ally. What alternative does it have? The alternative to Musharraf is another 'moderate' general like him – or worse – extremists, who would then have nuclear power in their hands.

The ongoing political unrest in Waziristan simultaneously highlights Pakistan's instability and implies that militants and the Taliban who are behind the increasing extremist violence in Afghanistan continue to frustrate Washington's campaign against terrorism. Musharraf remains caught in a bind. Threatened by extremists himself, yet unable to dispense with them against India, he has been accused by Ayman al-Zawahiri, the deputy Al Qaeda leader, of selling out to an Indo-American-Jewish combine which does not want a strong Pakistan.

He himself perceives the Indo-US nuclear agreement as 'disturbing' the balance of power in South Asia[5].

Meanwhile, it is unclear whether and how closer strategic ties between the US and India will contain terrorism.

The lesson from Pakistan – as from Iraq – is that the US cannot force liberal democracy on states or peoples. The military and clergy are too deeply entrenched in Pakistan's politics; the moulding of a less hostile perception of India may be a will o'the wisp.

Washington can press Musharraf to build coalitions with more moderate parties, but will he, if they question the army's cardinal role in Pakistani politics? His refusal to doff his uniform, despite a promise made to the opposition parties, suggests that he thinks that he can count on American support as he walks the political tightrope. But that implies that the US is ignoring or neglecting many causes of extremism in Pakistan. This could seriously diminish its ability to combat militant Islam not only in Afghanistan, but also in Iraq, and, more broadly, in the Middle East and Central Asia. Despite American talk of democratisation and reform with Pakistan could end up being counter-productive if it continues to make excuses for Pakistan's complicity in promoting extremism in the name of maintaining a strong alliance with its military elite. By refusing to govern without benefit of clergy, Musharraf and his army could spike America's guns against terrorism.

In South Asia, then, the US is countering terrorism through a military alliance with an illiberal Pakistan that stokes extremism; with a democratic India that shares its commitment to democratic values[8], and a fledgling democracy in Afghanistan. Both India and Afghanistan will continue to resist extremists educated and trained in Pakistan.

War, politics and diplomacy are not static; they are simultaneously arts of the possible and impossible. Is the US giving precedence to the short-term benefits of a military compact with Pakistan over its longer-term interests in containing terrorism? Can it cut the ground from under the feet of extremists if it is running with the hare and hunting with the hounds?

The means used to combat terrorism will create new ends – so what will replace terrorism? And how? Those are the questions the US, which will remain the primary political and military influence in South Asia, must address as it shapes its relationships with Afghanistan, Pakistan and India in the years to come. If democracy is to remain the legitimising ideology of the international system, the anti-terrorist strategies and tactics of the US in South Asia will impact on its global primacy, and establish whether it is the world's principal spoiler or a superpower bolstering the strength of the norms underpinning the international system, and of the capacity and legitimacy of international society to trounce terrorism.

Notes

1. Julian Borger, 'President Admits War on Terror Cannot be Won', *The Guardian,* 31 August 2004.

2. As urged by UN Secretary General Kofi Annan in his report, *In Larger Freedom, Towards Development, Security and Human Rights for All* (New York: United Nations, 2005), para. 91.

3. *A More Secure World: Our Shared Responsibility: Report of the High-Level Panel on Threats, Challenges and Changes* (New York: United Nations, 2004), para 146.

4. Inder Singh, *Democracy, Ethnic Diversity and Security.*

5. Sushant Sareen, 'War In Waziristan: Pakistan Faces a Serious Dilemma', *The Tribune*, 3 May 2006; BBC Report, 29 April 2006, http://news.bbc.co.uk./go/prfr/-/2/hi/middle_east/4957292,stm.

6. Manmohan Singh's stress on pluralism, ecularism, multi-culturalism and the principles of equity, social justice and the rule of law as the bedrock of India's democracy, and his assertion that India would be proud to identify with those who defend the values of liberal democracy and secularism across the world, strikes a chord with Secretary of State Condoleeza Rice's belief that closer Indo-US ties will be facilitated by the vibrancy of India's multi-ethnic democracy. On 26 May 2005, she explained how much that relationship had been transformed:

    'So India is a very key relationship here and we're spending a lot of time on it. When I went out there, we talked about a stronger economic relationship, stronger energy cooperation, stronger defence cooperation and becoming a reliable partner for India as it makes its move as a global power. And we used the words that we're fully willing and ready to assist in that growth of India's global power and the implications of that, which we see as largely positive.'

    Speech by Prime Minister Dr Manmohan Singh at India Today Conclave, New Delhi, February 25, 2005, http://www.pmindia.nic.in/pressrel.htm, and transcript to Condoleezza Rice's interview with Bloomberg News, http://usinfo.state.gov/usinfo/Archive/2005/May/26-750963.html.

Index

Abu Zubaydah, 48

141

144

145

149

Uzbeks, 32, 37
Taliban pressure, 15
Uzbekistan, 2, 13, 24
American Alliance, 8
Uzebekistan democracy
debate, 8

Vajpayee, A.B., 77, 80, 114, 116, 117

Vienna Declaration and
Programme of Action, 8
Voters in Afghanistan
militia threating, 31
Vyas, Sudhir, 107

Wall Street Journal, the, 52
Wardok, 37
Warloads
aim, 17
belligenrence, 22
bigger problem, 29
Cheking of traficking in
drugs, 19
control over local police and
intimidate election worker, 34
controlling the major customs
posts, 19
controlling the routs where
the opium transported to
foreign country, 19
extending their saway other
countries, 130
economic region, 18
ISAF presence in dealing, 34
ISAF troops failure of
dismantling, 30
Karzai fight, 33, 36
Karzai inclusion in his
government, 21
smuggling checking, 19
Tajik, 43
Uzbek, 43
Washington attack, 1-2, 14, 41
Waziristan, 56
Western bloc, 78
Women voters in Afghanistan
registration problem, 31-32
World Bank, 102
World Trade Centre attack, 1

Yeman, 53
Yigal Amir (Jewish Group, 7
Zia-ul-Haq, General, 47, 61, 67,
69, 111